THE QU

READING

Correcting Common Misreadings

ROMANS

Restoring Paul's Original Intent

RIGHT

KEITH GILES *and*
MATTHEW J. DISTEFANO

First Edition

Cover Design & Interior Layout by Matthew J. Distefano
Cover Image by Keith Giles

ISBN 978-1-964252-39-1

Printed in the United States of America

Published by Quoir
Chico, California
www.quoir.com

CONTENTS

FOREWORD

By Brandan Robertson

THE EPISTLE TO THE Romans is one of my favorite letters from the Apostle Paul. As a young, Reformed evangelical, I spent hours poring over this letter, inspired by Paul's profound spiritual insights about God's plan for the salvation of the world and the unique identity of Christians as a "chosen" people. For me and the pastors I learned from, Romans was the theological treatise of the New Testament, the cornerstone of our entire theology, and the groundwork for our understanding of the Gospel. In Romans, we believed we had Paul's expansive declaration of the sinfulness of humanity, his so-called condemnation of "homosexuality," some of the most poetic statements about the power of God's love, and a heartfelt message of hope in the sovereignty of God over all things.

Years later, as a progressive Christian and biblical scholar, I still find myself deeply intrigued and inspired by Paul's Epistle to the Romans. However, I now approach it with a very different understanding of its theology and implications for modern Christian life. It is remarkable how the lens through which we read this text can fundamentally change its message and implications. Instead of reading Paul through the lens of the Protestant Reformation—a framework that offered new interpretations of the letter roughly 1,500 years after it was written—I've learned to read Romans through the lens of Paul's apocalyptic, first-century Jewish worldview. Contextualizing this letter within the social, religious, and political nuances of the first-century Jewish world has unlocked even more profound insights and messages from Paul: God's faithfulness to redeem all people, sage guidance for how

Christians should engage politically and culturally, and the unique place of the Jewish people in Paul's understanding of God's redeeming work. Romans is truly a revolutionary theological text.

In biblical scholarship, a majority of scholars have long since rejected the "Reformed" view of Romans popularized by the Protestant Reformation. These scholars have sought to place Romans within its original culture, context, and theological paradigm, offering interpretations based on how its original recipients likely understood Paul's words. Yet, this scholarship has rarely made its way out of academic institutions and into the Church. As a result, the problematic, exclusionary, antisemitic, and thoroughly ahistorical interpretations of Romans promoted by the Protestant Reformers remain the primary way this text is understood by a vast majority of traditional Christians—Protestant and Catholic alike.

However, we live in an era of profound democratization of biblical scholarship. Through social media, podcasts, digital courses, and accessible books like this one, serious scholars, pastors, and thinkers are helping to deconstruct the so-called correct interpretations of biblical texts, especially Paul's writings. These efforts combat the problematic theology that continues to thrive due to a lack of understanding of the Bible's historical, cultural, and theological contexts.

Those with a vested interest in maintaining "traditional" interpretations of these texts often resist efforts to challenge their views through historical criticism and cultural contextualization. They believe their interpretations are historic and thus accurate, while any reinterpretation is seen as a distortion of the truth of Scripture. Their concern is understandable. When we re-engage the writings attributed to Paul—especially Romans—from a more scholarly and contextual perspective, foundational doctrines and theological paradigms of Reformed Christianity are inevitably called into question. This does not happen because scholars aim to distort the "truth" but because they are relentlessly committed to uncovering the truth. That truth is found not in the writings of John Calvin or Martin Luther but in the writings and records of first-century Jews and Christians, which we are privileged to study today.

In this accessible yet scholarly book, Keith and Matthew provide a careful engagement with the Epistle to the Romans, drawing on the best scholarship available. They are reliable and talented teachers who will guide you to see how drastically we have misunderstood Paul's letters. This misunderstanding has led to a version of Christianity that bears little resemblance to the faith Paul developed and Jesus inspired. Regardless of your background, your perspectives will be challenged, and you will be provoked to think about Romans in new ways. Ultimately, I believe you will be inspired by the power, relevance, and beauty of this letter. In a time when toxic teaching and poor Biblical scholarship are rampant in the Church, *Reading Romans Right* offers a necessary course correction that will transform your faith and equip you to reinterpret Paul's epistle with fresh eyes.

As you prepare to join Keith and Matthew in rereading Romans, take a moment to breathe deeply and center yourself. Be open to setting aside your preconceived ideas about the Apostle Paul and this famous epistle. Prepare to have your understanding expanded and your faith challenged in meaningful and helpful ways. If you are engaging with Romans for the first time, get ready for a theological tour de force through the most important theological text in Christianity. Its messages are profoundly relevant for our modern world, though many of its ideas deserve reevaluation. If you hold the Reformed and evangelical interpretation of Romans deep in your subconscious and have avoided re-engaging with this text because of those interpretations, prepare to have your theological boxes blown apart and the foundation laid for a truly prophetic, radical, and inclusive vision of the faith of Jesus and the earliest Christians.

Whoever you are, as you re-engage Romans with Keith and Matthew, prepare to be equipped to understand, engage with, and apply these powerful ancient words to your own faith and pursuit of justice in the modern world. Romans is a truly profound text, and this book will give you the tools to reclaim it from those who have weaponized it for far too long. Buckle up and prepare to be led on a transformative journey into this ancient letter of Paul by two of the finest voices in the field of public theology today.

PREFACE

KEITH AND I HAVE been friends and colleagues for over seven years, and business partners for close to three. While we have podcasted together for nearly a decade—shout out to all the *Heretic Happy Hour* listeners reading this book—this is our first co-authored work. I am not sure if that is surprising to any of you, but it sure comes as a shock to us.

Given this fact, an obvious question is raised: Why did we decide to kick off our co-authoring journey with, of all things, a book about the letter to the Romans? If you have listened to our very heretical podcast, you would know that Keith and I are not what anyone would consider "good Christians" any longer. So, why write a book about a book in *the* Book? It is simple, really: We are sick of the Epistle to the Romans being used as a justification for all sorts of bullshit (to use highly advanced and technical theological jargon).

First off, Romans 1:26–27 remains a favorite prooftext homophobes use to justify their bigotry. Males lying with males. Unnatural this and that. Yada, yada, yada. And then there is the "wrath of God" being revealed from heaven against those very same people and a God who literally hates people. Sorry, Mark Driscoll, but *make it make sense*. Romans 13 is then often cited as justification for Christian support of military action or police violence, and the necessity of empire in God's divine plan. When you step back and think about this letter, it really is a whopper of a conundrum!

But what if we in the Protestant tradition have been reading Romans erroneously this whole time? What if perhaps the greatest irony in American Christianity is that the bigots and homophobes are using this foundational letter all wrong—that Paul includes the hateful passages that seem to condemn others for *the sole purpose* of refuting the very same type of judgmental people later in the letter?

That will be our argument in this book.

No doubt, Calvinists and other fundamentalist Christians will bristle at such an idea. They have read Romans—and indeed the entire Bible—a *certain* way for their entire lives, and as we all know, changing our minds is hard. But that is what "repent" means in Greek—to change one's thinking—so it must be important! Maybe it is time Christians take such a concept seriously when it comes to their hermeneutics and indeed their very view of the Bible itself!

And speaking of the Bible—our plan with this book is to have it kick off an entire series where we, along with the help of our friends and colleagues, assist Christians in reading it right. And by "right," we do not mean right-wing. We also do not necessarily mean left-wing, though any accusation of "progressive" is not the burn conservative folks think it is. The opposite of progressive is regressive, so let us not even go there.

Nevertheless, that is the big goal of this series—to take a deep dive into the Bible. Keith and I will start with Romans, then plan on moving to Galatians, and, if *I* have my way, cover Genesis and Revelation. Once these four books are complete, we will then cast our net in the widest way possible, bringing on theologians and therapists, professors and prophets, and mystics and misfits to help all of us to read the entire Bible a little closer to "right."

If this Quoir Bible Series sounds interesting to you, then the book you have in your hand is just the beginning. But what a beginning it is! I mean, it *is* the letter to the Romans, after all—the pièce de resistance of the New Testament, the bee's knees of Christian theology, the magnum opus of Paul's writings. And while Romans has a lengthy history of being used to justify that which oppresses, marginalizes, ostracizes, and demonizes, it is our hope that this becomes a thing of the past, a hermeneutic relegated to the dustbin of an embarrassingly myopic Christian history.

So, please enjoy this book. The fact that you have it in your hand is already a sign that you are willing to expand your knowledge and grow in areas not all Christians are willing to go. We thank you for that, and hope that we can deliver an exhilarating and refreshing look at the letter some love to hate and others hate to love. We hope you enjoy *Reading Romans Right.*

— **MATTHEW J. DISTEFANO**
Chico, California
October 25, 2024

ACKNOWLEDGMENTS

We would like to thank the following people. In no particular order, they include:

Wendy Giles and Joyce Giles, for obvious reasons.

Lyndsay Distefano and Elyse Distefano, again, for obvious reasons.

Everyone who subscribes to the *Heretic Happy Hour* podcast or reads any of Quoir's books.

Douglas A. Campbell, Richard Beck, David Bentley Hart, Lucy Peppiatt, J. Louis Martyn, Chris Tilling, and Marcus Borg for helping us read Paul through a much clearer lens.

Michael Machuga for his friendship.

You, for having the audacity to read this book.

And finally, the Apostle Paul, for giving us something to talk about for 2,000 years.

"Neither a systematic theology nor a summary of Paul's lifework, [Romans] is by common consent his masterpiece. It dwarfs most of his other writings, an Alpine peak towering over hills and villages. Not all onlookers have viewed it in the same light or from the same angle, and their snapshots and paintings of it are sometimes remarkably unalike. Not all climbers have taken the same route up its sheer sides, and there is frequent disagreement on the best approach. What nobody doubts is that we are here dealing with a work of massive substance, presenting a formidable intellectual challenge while offering a breathtaking theological and spiritual vision."

N.T. WRIGHT
The New Interpreter's Bible

PART ONE

A Text Without a Context is a Con

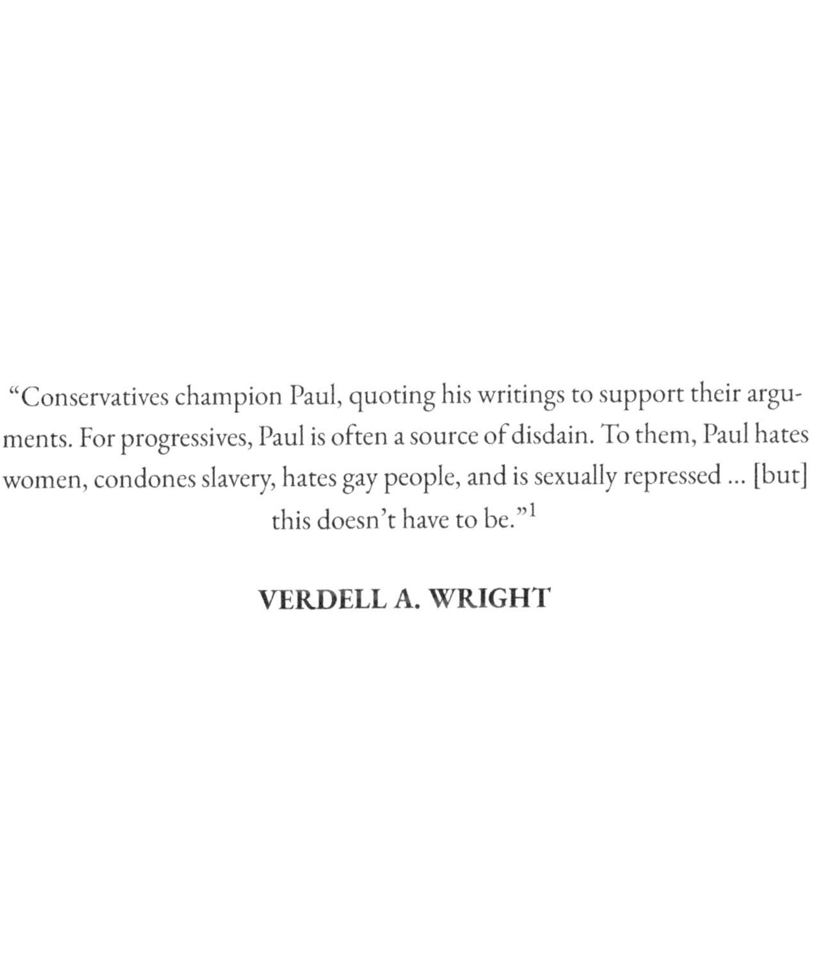

"Conservatives champion Paul, quoting his writings to support their arguments. For progressives, Paul is often a source of disdain. To them, Paul hates women, condones slavery, hates gay people, and is sexually repressed ... [but] this doesn't have to be."[1]

VERDELL A. WRIGHT

One

The Problem of the Apostle Paul

Who was Paul? A zealot? A misogynist? A homophobe? A wishy-washy intellectual who could never seem to make up his mind? Scholars have been debating these questions for a very long time. So, if you find yourself voraciously reading academic works on Paul, or if you yourself are in academia, you may not discover any *novel* bits of historical information about him in *this* volume (nor will that necessarily be our goal). It is not like either of us have found the *actual* first letter to the Corinthians,[1] nor have we stumbled upon a secret correspondence between Paul and some unknown lost lover (though it *would* be funny if *that* were his thorn in the flesh![2]).

What we will be doing, however, is presenting an understanding of Paul and his most influential letter that will be new to many lay Christians who have not read academics like Douglas A. Campbell, Chris Tilling, J. Louis Martyn, or Lucy Peppiatt (our personal favorite Pauline scholars). Though almost everything in this volume has been said before (by them and others), much (though not all) of it has been contained within the halls of prestigious colleges and universities.

Our job in this book is to help change that.

How we go about doing so will follow a typical back-and-forth "Matt and Keith" pattern.[3] At times our words will be biting, salty, and sarcastic—the parts typically written by Matthew—and in other instances, they will be imbued with love, empathy, and compassion—the parts generally written by Keith. And while we cannot foresee telling judgmental Christians to cut off their genitals,[4] given how many Calvinists have butchered Paul's sacred writings in the name of their own misogyny, racism, and homophobia, the temptation may persist over the course of this book.

Forgive us.

Now, as we just stated, it has been alleged that Paul was a terribly inconsistent thinker, no more so than when he is talking about his view of salvation in the Epistle to the Romans. As psychologist Richard Beck states:

> Pauline scholars have argued that Paul's soteriology, his view of salvation, is hopelessly muddled if not outright contradictory. To be sure, this might be unfair to both Paul and the canon. Paul might not be aiming for logical consistency. Plus, Paul might not have written everything we attribute to him. Regardless, it is worrying that Paul, the great theologian of the faith, might be confused or contradictory.[5]

While Beck is emphatically correct, Paul's inconsistencies and muddled writing style go well beyond the soteriology presented in the first eleven chapters of Romans. Peter, for instance, labels some things in Paul's writings, "hard to understand, which the ignorant and unstable twist to their own destruction, as they do the other scriptures,"[6] and it is not terribly difficult to understand why.

Throughout this book, it will be our contention that *that* is exactly what has happened to Paul—a twisting of his words—most notably by Calvinist TheoBros™ who would not know how to spot rhetoric if it were a Mike Tyson right hook to their biblically-bearded jaws. And while Paul's writings can in fact present us with *some* internal inconsistencies (even without the twisting by the ignorant), we will argue that the apostle is a much more reliable intellectual than what appears on the surface. We just need to know how to read him.

Nevertheless, in the following section, let us explore some of the ways in which Paul can be problematic, where we may discover some of his thorniest ideas, and where he seems to contradict himself. Only then can we lay the groundwork for how we can go about approaching his most theologically important, yet too often misunderstood letter (and the main topic of this book): *the Epistle to the Romans.*

DIFFICULTIES ABOUND

Problem #1: The Phenomenology of Paul

Like everyone in the Bible—and indeed everyone who has ever lived—Paul was a human being having a subjective human experience. Meaning: Paul viewed everything through his own lens and we need to allow him the space to develop as a thinker, as a writer, and as a theologian. (After all, no one is born with perfect theology, nor do they ever develop it.[7]) For example, if Paul's eschatology shifts sometime between 1 Thessalonians and Romans—which it assuredly does—then we need to allow for such a change, rather than trying to make *everything* "fit."[8] These are letters, after all, coming from a man who undergoes *quite a transformation*. To begin, his upbringing leads him to become as devoutly religious as imaginable. In his own words, his history is that of, "a Hebrew born of Hebrews; as to the Law, a Pharisee; as to zeal, a persecutor of the church; as to righteousness under the Law, blameless."[9] Then ... bam! The Damascus Road event, where everything seems to start anew.

Well, not exactly everything!

First, Paul never stops being a Jew. When he is confronted by the risen Christ on the road to Damascus, he does *not* convert from Judaism to Christianity. After all, the Jesus' story is a decidedly Jewish one! Paul's "conversion" is from a violent zealot to a nonviolent (yet shrewd and sarcastic) activist type who would go on to view everything through Christ's death and resurrection.

Second, contrary to popular myth, Paul does *not* ever change his name from Saul. It may be a nice symbolic shift for us to think about, but it has no bearing on the historicity of the event.

As far as Paul's understanding of God and what righteousness *truly* means, however, his face-to-face encounter with the risen Christ kickstarts a change in everything. The philosophical and theological development of thought that follows obviously takes time to catch up, though. In other words, the profundity of the event takes decades to fully work its way throughout Paul's entire worldview, as it likely would for any of us.[10] And so, as we move through time, from Galatians to Romans, a lot of Paul's thinking shifts, which is only the *beginning* of the complexities of his letters.

Problem #2: The Question of Authenticity

The second issue we run into with Paul is that some letters attributed to him are not "authentic." In fact, of the thirteen "Pauline epistles," the consensus among most scholars is that only seven are penned by the apostle: Galatians, Romans, 1 Corinthians, 2 Corinthians, Philemon, Philippians, 1 Thessalonians. Three of the epistles are generally seen as pseudepigraphic: 1 Timothy, 2 Timothy, and Titus. The remaining three are often debated, but are likely written by a disciple or follower of Pauline thought: 2 Thessalonians, Ephesians, and Colossians (one of Keith's favorites). Anyone who still believes Paul wrote Hebrews is not a serious scholar.

Why is this important?

One reason is that while Paul can indeed present a conundrum when it comes to women and the LGBTQ+ community, most of the anti-egalitarian language comes from the pseudepigraphic epistles of 1 and 2 Timothy and Titus. Not that that fact completely recuses Paul of his potential misogyny and shortsightedness—those epistles can still be found in the Bible, and were written by his "understudies"—it at least gives us a bit more context. If we are going to take people at their word, we need to primarily hold them accountable for the verifiable things they have said and written, not the things we now know they did not. Paul should be no exception.

Problem #3: Patriarchy, Misogyny, and Contradictory Messaging

Speaking of Paul's misogyny, on the surface it seems to come in spades. However, as we just stated, much of it comes, not from Paul, but from some disciple/s of Paul. Again, we *can* assume they got their troubling views from the apostle himself, but we should at least acknowledge Paul did not write the epistles that are the most egregious in their misogyny.

1 Corinthians, on the other hand, *was* written by Paul and indeed contains some troubling anti-woman passages; but if we follow Lucy Peppiatt's thesis, much of the same style of rhetoric that takes place in Romans—the topic of *this* book—also occurs in the Corinthian letters.[11] Meaning: some of the misogyny is really Paul quoting (often sarcastically) those he is in heated debate with. Think of it like *The Colbert Report*, where the satirist Stephen Colbert plays a conservative talk show host whose whole point is to act as a rhetorical device *against* conservatism. And so, just like it would be dubious to quote Colbert unironically, it is sometimes even more so to quote Paul the same way.

And yet, we can safely say Paul *is* a product of his time and assuredly had what we now understand to be harmful views of women. He also seemed to believe marriage was for the weak. Further, perhaps he may have thought it best for women to "keep the home." And lastly, we are also confident he would not view what we now call "healthy sexuality" all too favorably. But one thing he did get profoundly correct early on in his writings is this: there should be no religious, social, or gender dividing lines in the body of Christ.[12] Applied to today's context, Paul can also be viewed as quite the progressive—ironic, given how many conservatives use Paul for their myopic arguments.

Problem #4: Paul's View of Salvation

Given the gravity of the topic and how it relates to Christian theology at large, one of the biggest points of contention among Pauline scholars is how salvation (soteriology) is achieved. If a reader turns to Romans 1–4, they will get a very different picture than if they turn to Romans 5–8. In the former, salvation is contractual—the perfect example of a *quid pro quo*! Everyone begins in a "pre-saved" phase and only through accepting the "blood sacrifice" of Jesus—i.e., a contract inked in blood—can one pass into the "saved" phase. Romans 5–8, on the other hand, is more "apocalyptic." That is, God reveals that which was once hidden by breaking into the world through Christ, and delivers every square inch of it in a kind of heroic rescue mission, walking off into the sunset like a badass.

The revelation of Christ is that we are "saved" through *his* act of righteousness, and of *no* accord of our own. And sure, it is better to know the truth than not to, but our *not* knowing does *not* change the certainty of what is. Jesus Christ rescues everyone from "sin and death," so hop on board or do not; in the end, everyone will eventually know the truth that what was done "in Adam" has been undone "in Christ."[13]

More will be said about the apocalyptic view in later chapters, but it brings us to a crucial point: what do we even mean by "salvation?" In Judaism during the Second Temple period, the individualistic Western notion of "personal salvation" would have been a bit of a misnomer. Deliverance would not have been coming so much to individual Jews; deliverance would have been coming for "the People"—not "I" and "thou," but "we." Occupation in all its forms was going to come to an end, thanks to the messiah. Babylon. Rome. It did not matter; *"the nations" were going to get their comeuppance and Israel was going to get delivered.*

Turning to modern-day Protestantism, and within many denominations the *individual* is over-emphasized while the community is pooh-poohed as some kind of "communist gobbledygook." Christians have their "personal

Lord and Savior." They have their "personal relationship with Christ." And "the whole" is forever divided between "the saved"—always "us"—and the damned—always "them." That is why, when we Western folks turn to Paul's writings, we typically bring *that* egocentric lens along for the ride, pervasively reading ourselves into the text as if the letters were addressed to us.

Throughout this book, we will attempt to divorce ourselves from such a narcissistic hermeneutic for the sake of meeting Paul on his own *Jewish* terms, namely one that speaks of salvation primarily in terms of "the whole."

Problem #5: The Meaning of Pistis Christou

The last issue we want to briefly mention in this chapter piggybacks off problem #4, and involves the debate over the meaning of the Greek phrase "*pistis Christou*" (πίστις χριστοῦ) from Romans 3:21–22. For "old school" Christians like R.C. Sproul, "faith *in* Christ" is the most accurate translation, while "new school" theologians like N.T. Wright and David Bentley Hart argue that the "faithfulness *of* Christ" is more precise.[14] Why does this matter? It matters because the key difference—*in* vs. *of*—could be the deciding factor between whether whole swaths of people are under Christ's salvific act or not. Rest assured, we will explore this passage more in Part Three, but for now let us just say this: though we cannot know with one-hundred percent assurance, the more consistent message from Paul is that we should emphasize Christ and *his* faith over any semblance of personal belief *in* him. In other words, we are team Wright and DBH, because to our minds, if we are going to err on the side of anything, it would be to overemphasize Christ's role in salvation while underemphasizing ours—especially given how pessimistic Paul's view of the human will is and how accentuated Christ is throughout the whole of Pauline thought.

IN CLOSING

As we move forward throughout this book, please keep in mind these important contextual considerations. No matter what we believe about Paul, or the Bible for that matter, we must meet the writers on their own terms as we tease out the "meaning" of the text (exegesis). Anachronisms are tempting, but refraining from them is crucial if we want to get to the heart of what an ancient writer like Paul was attempting to convey. Otherwise, we do nothing but speak for them, inserting our own context into the text (eisegesis).

In the following chapter, we are going to dive deeper into the "standard" Protestant formula for how one experiences salvation, breaking down all the intrinsic, systemic, and empirical problems that come with it. In doing so, our goal will be to set the stage for a way of reading Romans without these faulty presuppositions. But that will be reserved for parts Two and Three. Now, it is time to undo some of the assumptions we have made about how salvation "works." It is time to tackle the doctrine of Justification Theory.

Two

Traditional Justification Theory and Its Many Pitfalls

In chapter 1, we touched on the excessively personal nature of salvation within the western Christian mindset. However, that is not the only issue with what we will be calling Justification Theory. Relying heavily on *The Deliverance of God* by Pauline scholar Douglas A. Campbell, this chapter will explore three categories of problems that arise from this model: intrinsic, systemic, and empirical.

Before we do that, however, let us reiterate that what we will be exploring is predominantly a Protestant problem, as Catholics and Eastern Orthodox folks do not typically hold to the views herein. The reason being that Justification Theory is tied to modernity. It relies on the so-called autonomous self, which did not come into fashion until *after* Kant and the Enlightenment. Catholic and Orthodox theology predates such a philosophical movement by over 1,500 years—sorry to break it to you, Mrs. Childers![1] Not that this fact makes them *necessarily* correct—Catholics and Orthodox disagree on plenty—we just need to remember that modern Protestantism is, 1) a product of *post*-biblical, *post*-Enlightenment thinking and, 2) not the default position of most Christians throughout history (or even today).

Nevertheless, because this problematic view persists throughout many of our American churches, let us spend the rest of the chapter dismantling it brick by brick, so that, beginning in Part Two, we can reconstruct something much sturdier.

Before we can do that, however, let us put forward a more robust definition of Justification Theory so everyone can track what we will be exploring throughout this chapter.

WHAT IS JUSTIFICATION THEORY?

Put most simply, Justification Theory is a rationalistic[2] two-step prospective[3] process a minority of people (Christians) take to move from a pre-saved to a saved phase. While most folks arguably stay in phase 1 (unsaved), the elect (whether through their own free will[4] or God's monergistic act[5]), move from phase 1 to phase 2 through *faith alone*.

For this introspective[6] process to work, two things must first be realized: 1) sinners must acknowledge there exists a retributive God who will get his justice for sin—think of God like *The Godfather* instead of God the Father—and, 2) there is nothing a person can do to assuage God and his wrath. As it was for *The Office's* Michael Scott when he realized Dunder Mifflin was filing for bankruptcy and exclaimed, "It's over, we are screwed," so it is for self-interested[7] sinners who can grasp both points above.[8] When this happens, though emotional despair inevitably takes hold—that's part of the driving force—there is a contractual[9] escape offered: the substitutionary sacrifice of God's son, Jesus of Nazareth. If, by faith, one accepts the *quid pro quo* and believes that the two-thousand-year-old lynching of God's son washes their sin away, then they are imputed with righteousness (i.e., saved).

If that is too verbose a description, allow us to rather sarcastically consolidate the story:

> We are all, by default, wretched worms in need a savior, so God sent himself in the form of his son to kick the ever-loving hell out of himself so he could unlock the mechanism needed to spare some of us from the shit-kicking that was supposed to come our way. Those who accept the grotesque blood sacrifice

> and have faith in Christ will one day find themselves in heaven with that very same God, while those who do not will wind up in hell, writhing around in blistering agony, forever separated from love in all its forms.

Sick stuff, we know ... so take a moment to pause if you need.

Better?

Okay.

Before we move on to the fatal problems of this psychologically tormenting story, here is a graphic for our more visually-minded readers:

JUSTIFICATION THEORY

Pre-Saved Phase

Key Realizations

1. God's justice is retributive (fear)
2. You cannot save yourself from God's wrath (emotional despair)

Torah Obedience — Jews

Natural Moral Law — Gentiles

FAITH

Saved Phase

Key Element

Continued belief in the substitutionary sacrifice of Jesus

Key Characteristics

1. Rationalistic
2. Prospective
3. Introspective
4. Self-Interested
5. Contractual

THE MULTI-FACETED PROBLEMS OF JUSTIFICATION THEORY

Intrinsic

Campbell labels the first set of problems "intrinsic" because they involve difficulties with the theory *as a theory*—the coherence of the theory as such. For example, on the one hand, Justification Theory relies on the fact that phase 1 sinners can take an honest look at the universe, and through some sort of natural revelation,[10] rationalistically determine their need for a savior from a retributive God; but on the other hand, these same sinners are so utterly corrupt that they can do nothing good on their own.[11] How can that be? If sinners are so corrupt in the pre-saved phase, how can they also acknowledge their need for salvation from *within* this phase? Or, as Campbell frames it: "How do these contradictory tendencies coexist within the same account of humanity?—the capacity to discern the good, to do it, and to be held accountable for it, combined with an inevitable and repeated sinfulness."[12] To our minds, a completely corrupt sinner void of divine revelation would always dig in their heels; that is definitional by the theory's own terms, and is perhaps one reason Campbell goes on to label the anthropology of this model "fundamentally incoherent" and "garbled."[13]

We could not agree more.

However, for the sake of argument, let us imagine some of these very same sinners *indeed* receive a divine revelation and move from phase 1 to phase 2—what of those who do not? They are Gentiles who have looked at the "natural moral truths and law" of the universe, concluded that there must be a God who demands justice and realized their need for a savior from such punishment, but one never comes. The message fails to be delivered by human hands. Or, worse yet, a distorted message is delivered by the blood-soaked hands of one of the many abusive, misogynist, homophobic, predatory, patriarchal pastors and priests Christianity has produced over the centuries. What happens then? Given Justification Theory's resounding lack of empathy with regards to questions like this, we shudder to think.

Further, why does the God of this scenario require one-hundred percent perfection ... *or else?* Why is there an eternal hell awaiting sinners *at all*? And why is the punishment—eternal separation from God—the exact same for those who are morally perfect ninety-nine percent of the time and those who are sociopathic serial killers all the time?[14] Moreover, why are flawed humans held to such an impossibly high standard for simply doing that which sinners are designed and destined to do? God made us this way, so why are *we* to blame? The Ford Motor Company does not get to blame the infamously terrible Pinto vehicle for being an unreliable piece of junk, so why does the Creator of the universe get to eternally blame us for not living up to a standard only he can achieve? The answer, one must say, is that for Justification Theory to at least have some semblance of internal logic, everyone needs to stand universally *condemned* before a wrathful God. Without this, there would be no need for a savior called Jesus. Sinners would be able to potentially do the work on their own, and then the whole theory would fall to the floor like a house made of playing cards.

Phenomenologically, of course, none of this makes sense. No good and decent person requires one-hundred-percent perfection of their loved ones ... *or else*. And no good judge in any court doles out infinitely harsh, supra-retributive punishment, no matter how heinous the crime. In the United States—a kingdom that pales in comparison to the kingdom of God—even *we* have a law that says there shall be no "cruel and unusual punishments," yet everlasting hell for a finite number of sins violates both stipulations we all agree are required for fair judgments. And here we thought God was a fair judge! There is nothing intrinsically fair about this model of salvation.

Systemic

The second set of problems Campbell identifies are "systemic" because they cause systemic issues within Paul himself, transforming the apostle into the very same contradictory theologian we touched on in chapter 1. In Campbell's own words:

> If the essentially contractual theory of Justification is inserted into Paul's thought, then almost every aspect generates tension in relation to something the apostle says elsewhere—a complaint with a long pedigree within Pauline scholarship.[15]

For instance, as we explored earlier, if we compare the soteriology from Romans 1–4 to that of 5–8, we will notice an obvious contrast that is impossible to reconcile (though many conservative apologists have tried). Due to this fact, the simple conclusion is one of two things: either Paul is an inconsistent thinker or he is not teaching soteriology in both places.

Because if he is consistent then here is the first problem in detail: In Romans 1–4, sinners must look inward at their own wretchedness, cry out for a savior, and then manifest something called "faith" to be saved. On the other hand, Romans 5–8 is essentially a rescue mission by God to save sinners. Full stop. There is nothing we inwardly must do. Rather, the *apocalypse of Christ* reveals God's plan of salvation for all who are "in Adam."[16]

This contradiction is not the only issue, however. Below are five others:

1. Justification Theory is a rationalistic exercise that prospectively leads sinners from phase 1 to phase 2, while in the apocalyptic view from Romans 5–8, God delivers all sinners from sin and death, thus giving them clarity over their situation by allowing them to look *back* at what once was (or to their pre-*rescued* status).

2. In Justification Theory, God's justice is retributive, while in the apocalyptic view, God is, to use Beck's phrasing, "wholly benevolent."[17]

3. There is no ethical point to the theory of Justification. One's salvation is simply hell avoidance and "sanctification" supposedly follows. However, once in phase 2, nothing within the model of Justification itself drives people toward becoming more Christlike. With the apocalyptic view, however, in being rescued by Christ from "sin and death," liberation becomes our motivation by becoming our mimetic model—that is, we follow Christ because he *first showed us* how to live and move and be in the world.[18]

4. Justification Theory overemphasizes Christ's death as being a punishment for sin—the more Calvinistic the church, the bloodier the sermons and song lyrics—while elsewhere in Paul's writings, the death of Jesus is the universal "termination of a sinful condition."[19] The resurrection, then, is the proof that God does not engage in retributive punishment; instead, the Father brings life by rejecting *our* violence.

5. Justification Theory requires no universal church whatsoever. Rather, movement from phase 1 to phase 2 is entirely individualistic. What happens to "you" is none of "my" concern within this system. However, given that the apocalyptic model is universal—*what was done "in Adam" has been undone "in Christ"*[20]—the church has the capacity to be universal as well, should it follow God's lead and include ... wait for it ... literally *all people*—everyone who was once "in Adam" but who are now "in Christ."[21]

Empirical

Finally, as Campbell admits, while empirical data regarding biblical and theological theories is generally hard to come by, since a part of Justification Theory includes its historical claims about what Second Temple Judaism looked like in the first century, there are some things we *can* test.

According to Justification Theory, the Judaism of Jesus and Paul's day was monolithically "rigid," "strict," and forced a legalized adherence to Torah—that is how Jews experienced the emotional torment that would cause them to acknowledge their need for a savior. However, there is no other way to say this except that it is historically untrue. Overall, Jews were not typically working from a place of legalism—though obviously the Judaizers were—but did believe they had a covenant with God and a duty to live up to their end of the bargain.

Second, Justification Theory fails miserably in accounting for anyone's personal experience that does not fit within the prescribed formula laid out in the earlier graphic. In other words, if a Christian's conversion from phase 1 to phase 2 does not go according to the two-step process, Protestants are likely to throw it out. "Sorry, but it must not count," they would likely say.[22] There is no way of getting around the fact that Justification Theory posits how *all* sinners who are "called" will come to a spiritually and emotionally tormented place where they recognize their need for a savior; and when they do, will be so struck by their shame and guilt that they will turn from their sin and toward God. And while this story may be true for some people, it is certainly not true for all Christians. We doubt if it is true for anything close to a majority, let alone a universal fact that can be traced throughout the entirety of Christian history. Thus, Justification Theory falls apart the moment we consider all the testimonies from those who simply have not experienced what *must* be experienced for the theory to hold any water.

IN CLOSING

So, now that we have processed through some of the key problems with the theory of Justification, let us move forward and begin tackling the reason we are all here: the epistle to the Romans. While this letter is not an easy one to read or comprehend, it is our contention that by the end of Part Two, you will be well on your way to having the proper framework from which to work. Part Three, then, will be a deep dive into the text itself, where we will offer a new way of digesting all the theologically dense material.

Starting in the next chapter, we will first take a closer look at the traditional way of reading Romans 1–4, and how most "old school" theologians consolidate the obviously disparate ideas between these chapters and the four that follow. Next, we will introduce the backdrop of the apocalyptic view, why Paul's firsthand account of the risen Christ fits within this reading, and how Paul's post-conversion nonviolence should be the lens through which to view soteriology, before finally closing out Part Two by offering a 30,000-foot view of the apocalyptic reading of Romans, introducing terms like *prosopopoeia* and *diatribe*, and arguing that no serious reader should pluck any verse from Romans 1–11 without understanding the entire thrust of the argument at hand.

With that said, sit back and buckle your seatbelts because the fun has just begun. Let us dive into the traditional reading of Romans 1–4 and explain why it is a less than compelling way of understanding the pivotal text proponents of Justification Theory use, before moving on to a much more exciting and historical model—the apocalyptic reading of Romans.

PART TWO

An Introduction to the Epistle to the Romans

"This epistle is really the chief part of the New Testament, and is truly the purest gospel. It is worthy not only that every Christian should know it word for word, by heart, but also that he should occupy himself with it every day, as the daily bread of the soul. We can never read it or ponder over it too much; for the more we deal with it, the more precious it becomes and the better it tastes."

MARTIN LUTHER

Luther's Works, Volume 35

Three

The Traditional Reading of Romans 1–4

Before we begin our introduction to the traditional reading of Romans—and again, by "traditional" we mean by Protestant standards—we need to get some of the nuts and bolts of the epistle out of the way. Call them the Wikipedia highlights, if you must:

- Romans is the sixth book in the New Testament, and the longest of all of Paul's letters.

- There was early circulation among Christians of a version of Romans with only fourteen or fifteen chapters.

- Likely transcribed by Terius while Paul was staying with Gaius in the Greek city of Corinth, the letter is dated between late 55 CE and early 57 CE.

- A deacon (*diákonos*) named Phoebe was the deliverer of the letter (putting to bed the notion that women could not obtain leadership roles under Paul's theology).

- Of the seven authentic Pauline letters, Romans is the fifth oldest, probably written after 2 Corinthians and before Philippians.

- The letter is likely written because of Paul's ambition to preach the gospel in Spain (Rome would have been on the way from Greece).

- Churches in Rome were composed of both Jews and Gentiles, as Judaism had a substantial presence in the city.
- Contrary to what second-century Church father Irenaeus said, Paul did not establish any churches in Rome (unlike he did in the city of Galatia).

With the basic facts of the letter covered, let us kick off this part of the book by jumping headlong into the text itself. First, throughout this chapter, we will "attack the citadel" of Justification Theory (as Campbell puts it), before moving on to the apocalyptic reading championed by Campbell, Tilling, and Peppiatt in the following one.

BREAKING DOWN THE "OLD SCHOOL" READING

A Problem That Demands a Solution: Romans 1:18-3:20

After Paul greets the Romans, provides some introductory notes, and offers a prayer of thanksgiving, the apostle gets into the meat of the letter. His goal in these first few chapters, according to the traditionalists, is to build a case that all are under the "wrath of God" because "*all have sinned and fall short of the glory of God*" (3:23). He does this by separating the Roman Christians into two groups: Gentiles and Jews.

Beginning with the Gentiles in 1:18–2:8, Paul lays out all the ways in which they stand condemned and thus under God's ire, informing them that they should have known better through "naturalistic" means:

> Ever since the creation of the world God's eternal power and divine nature, invisible though they are, have been seen and

> understood through the things God has made. So they are without excuse, for though they knew God, they did not honor him as God or give thanks to him, but they became futile in their thinking, and their senseless hearts were darkened (1:20–21).

What Paul is saying here is fairly cut and dried: God's presence in this world is so obvious that Gentile Christians in Rome have no valid excuses for rejecting him. Plain and simple, they stand condemned before the God of Abraham, Jacob, and Isaac, even if they have never heard these names before. Their punishment? The eternal wrath of God poured out on them.

Paul's fellow Jews are not let off the hook, however. Being a "Hebrew of Hebrews," the apostle turns to the Torah to show how *they* too are all condemned. By making this move, Paul is reminding the Jewish Christians in Rome that "through the Law" they have become conscious of sin (3:20). Whereas Gentiles have had to look to the "things God has made" to understand his "eternal power and divine nature," Jews have had it a bit easier by possessing the Law of Moses this whole time. That is why Paul indicts both groups in the following way: "There will be affliction and distress for everyone who does evil, both the Jew *first* and the Greek" (2:9, emphasis ours).

And so, according to the "traditional" reading, the problem is reiterated like this: *All have sinned and fall short of the glory of God* (3:23), *all should know this*—Gentiles through "natural" means (1:20–21), Jews through knowledge of and adherence to the law (3:20)—*thus all stand con demned before an eternal God of wrath* (1:18).

A Solution to the Problem: Romans 1:16-17, 3:21-31

If there is a problem, there must be a solution. Both Jews and Gentiles stand condemned, and as such, risk facing God's wrath. So, Paul's answer is that through "faith in Jesus Christ," all who believe will receive the blessings of God's righteousness (3:22). That is the gospel in which the traditionalists say Paul is not ashamed, the "good news" that has "saving power for everyone who believes, for the Jew *first* and also for the Greek" (1:16–17, emphasis ours).

For scriptural support, Paul turns to the father of the Hebrew people, pointing out how it was Abraham's faith, and nothing more, that was credited to him as righteousness (4:1–3)—long before the Torah (i.e., the Law) had been given to Moses! This is the same "faith *in* Christ" Paul states will be credited to believers (3:22), connecting the historic with the "modern" in a creative exegetical move that, if not in the Bible, would otherwise leave modern Calvinists aghast.[1]

THE EXEGETICAL, THEOLOGICAL, AND ANTHROPOLOGICAL DIFFICULTIES WITH A TRADITIONAL READING

On the surface, this "traditional" reading makes a lot of sense. For those of us who grew up in the Protestant tradition, it is perhaps the only version of the story we heard, so it is a narrative much more noteworthy for us. However, there are a litany of problems with this reading, which we have already alluded to in this book. In this section, we would like to cover four of them much more in depth.

Textual Underdeterminations and Overdeterminations

When picking apart the text from which the theory of Justification derives (Romans 1–4), we notice two initial types of problems. First, we have textual underdeterminations—these happen when the theory says more than what is in the text itself. In other words, Justification Theory's suppositions must be read *into the text* (eisegesis) because they simply are not found in there. Second are textual overdeterminations—these happen when the text says more than the theory posits. When this occurs, textual information may go unnoticed and often even contradicts the theory itself.

A few of the most noteworthy examples of where under- and overdeterminations occur are as follows:

1. Underdetermination: Justification Theory states that God demands one-hundred percent moral perfection ... *or else!* This is why there is nothing sinners can do to assuage the eternal wrath of God. Jesus, as God's Son, is one-hundred percent morally perfect, so must be sent to achieve this on our behalf. However, when Paul condemns both Jew and Gentile alike, he does not include this very important bit of information—a strict, complete moral adherence to God's Law must be read into both the text and, more broadly speaking, Judaism itself.[2]

   Thus, Justification Theory overstates the nature of a sinner's relationship to moral perfection and the Jewish Law.

2. Underdetermination: In Justification Theory, all stand universally condemned—Jews and Gentiles alike. Thus, when proponents of the traditional reading of Romans turn to 2:1, they automatically universalize the Jewish person/s mentioned in the passage. In other words, the "you" Paul is admonishing becomes a stand-in for "Judaism as such."[3] However, this is simply not found in the text itself (in fact, quite the opposite!). As Campbell points out, "Paul never states explicitly in Romans 1:18–3:20 that he is criticizing Jews and Judaism per se, and thereby himself, presumably in his former life. The text only ever criticizes a Jew—a learned, judgmental male."[4]

Thus, Justification Theory overstates the scope of the hypocritical figure in Romans 2:1, conflating a particular male Jew/s with all of Judaism.

3. Overdetermination: In Justification Theory, humans are divided neatly into two generalized groups: the righteous and the wicked. In Romans 2:6–10, a traditional reading pits these two groups against each other and are described as follows: the righteous "patiently do good, seeking glory and honor," while the wicked are "self-seeking who obey injustice." However, in the real world, this is overly reductive and plainly untrue. As Campbell puts it, "no one is monolithically good or bad in terms of deeds."[5] Or, as Russian author Aleksandr Solzhenitsyn once stated, "The line separating good and evil passes not through states, nor between classes, nor between political parties either—but right through every human heart—and through all human hearts."[6] Further, if the whole problem is that, "all sin and fall short of the glory of God" (3:23), then why separate these two groups in such a reductively deed-based and dichotomous way?

   Thus, a traditional reading of Romans 1–4 overstates the moral aptitude of the righteous, while reductively caricaturizing the wickedness of the damned.

4. Overdetermination: Regardless of our preferred reading of Romans, no one can deny that 1:18–32 is essentially a remix of Wisdom of Solomon, a book full of anti-Gentile propaganda.[7] If the traditional reading is true, then, why would Paul borrow from such a book, painstakingly and approvingly quote from it, only to turn around and denounce those who hypocritically do the same? A traditional reading of 1:18–2:1 makes Paul out to be a "crude and harsh" preacher who both A) agrees with the sentiment from

Wisdom of Solomon (and by extension Romans 1:18–32), and B) disagrees with all of Judaism for having such views in the first place.[8] This makes Paul out to be a wildly inconsistent theologian and perhaps even a blatant hypocrite.

Thus, a traditional reading of Romans 1–4, which uses anti-Gentile propaganda from the Wisdom of Solomon, is both used by Paul and denounced by him, and Justification Theory fails to account for such a contradiction.

The Gospel of "Old Paul"

In chapter 1, we mentioned the firsthand account of Paul's Damascus Road transformation. In this section, we would like to revisit this event and expand on those cursory thoughts.

First, the problem with pre-conversion Paul is not his personal adherence to the Law; it is that his adherence to the Law is used to justify his ostracization and subsequent violence against others. That is, Paul's faith was defined by those who were "in" and those who were "out"—and those who were "out" often got the business end of a spear or sword. With the traditional reading, Christians of all kinds follow in this tradition, reading themselves into the text as "Jacob" instead of "Esau," as the saved instead of the damned, as the righteous instead of the wicked. Then, some of these Christians look down upon nonbelievers and even commit violence against them in the same way pre-conversion Paul did.

The irony is not lost on us.

To that end, if the traditional reading is the correct one, obvious questions are raised: Did Paul's "conversion" mean nothing to him? Or, did that fateful day on the Damascus Road just change the qualifiers of those who are "in" and those who are "out," a categorical reorganization that fails to cut to the heart of the issue in the first place—violence and othering? Justification

Theory suggests the latter is the clearer choice, while experiential knowledge and common sense suggest the former is more in line with reality.

This disconnect becomes an immense problem for proponents of the traditional reading. On the one hand, we have very specific and detailed knowledge of a great amount of historical information about Paul, including a contextual backstory with a conversion of epic proportions, but then are left with a reading of his most important epistle that seems to account for none of this. We expect a massive theological change in Paul, but as we read him through traditionally Protestant eyes, we see much more of the same—a dualistic thinker whose theology fails to line up with the real-world experiences of so many of his fellow Christians.

The Gospel of Homophobia

Any run-of-the-mill bigot's favorite prooftext against the LGBTQ+ community must come from Romans 1:18–32, specifically verses 26–27, so it would behoove us to cover them here:

> For this reason God gave them over to dishonorable passions. Their females exchanged natural intercourse for unnatural, and in the same way also the males, giving up natural intercourse with females, were consumed with their passionate desires for one another. Males committed shameless acts with males and received in their own persons the due penalty for their error.

On the surface, this sounds like a hearty critique of "homosexuality,"[9] a cut-and-dried case of "the Bible clearly says." However, major problems abound with such a reading.

First, "homosexuality" is not a concept in the first century. At least, not according to the *Oxford Classical Dictionary*, which states:

> No Greek or Latin word corresponds to the modern term homosexuality, and ancient Mediterranean societies did not in practice treat homosexuality as a socially operative category of personal or public life. Sexual relations between persons of the same sex certainly did occur (they are widely attested in ancient sources), but they were not systematically distinguished or conceptualized as such, much less were they thought to represent a single, homogeneous phenomenon in contradistinction to sexual relations between persons of different sexes. That is because the ancients did not classify kinds of sexual desire or behavior according to the sameness or difference of the sexes of the persons who engaged in a sexual act; rather, they evaluated sexual acts according to the degree to which such acts either violated or conformed to norms of conduct deemed appropriate to individual sexual actors by reason of their gender, age, and social status ... the application of "homosexuality" (and "heterosexuality") in a substantive and normative sense to sexual expression in classical antiquity is not advised.[10]

Second, any commentator who argues that the passage in question denounces being gay as such, or even "gay sex," is again engaging in yet another textual underdetermination. In this case, the theory would state that Paul is denouncing "gay sex," but what Paul really says is that men and women gave up "natural" sex for "unnatural," and that these acts are "shameful." He does not necessarily define what these acts are or what exactly makes them shameful. To suggest it is shameful simply because of its same-gendered nature is to engage in blatant eisegesis.

In the ancient world, what must be understood is that often, male-male sex happened in the context of power, dominance, coercion, control, and religious ritualistic worship. One might call this *idolatry*. Put simply: well-to-do older Roman men are known to have raped younger, poorer boys, often as a religious rite tied to whatever god/s they worshipped. Hence, the rules for their sexual engagements are skewed toward one party at the expense of the other, all in the name of the divine. It can easily be argued that this is what Paul is denouncing, rather than gay sex as such (more on this in chapter 5).

Lastly, if Paul is indeed being "homophobic"—a gross anachronism, given the above quote from the *Oxford Classical Dictionary*—then we are again presented with a systemic problem within Paul. On the one hand, Paul would be creating dividing lines between "gay" and "straight," yet in other places he says that in the body of Christ, there are to be no such demarcations: "There is no longer Jew or Greek; there is no longer slave or free; there is no longer male or female, for all of you are one in Christ Jesus."[11]

And sure, Paul does not specifically use the terms "gay" and "straight" here. How could he? But if his philosophy is to hold, these modern sociological classifications could not be pitted against one another without violating the rules of his own game, which he states explicitly as follows: "for all of you are *one* in Christ Jesus." (emphasis ours)

The Gospel of Wrath

One key component of Justification Theory is the wrath of God. Often used interchangeably with the "justice of God," divine wrath is a concept that has been hotly debated for ages. Some Christians—the Pipers and Driscolls of the world—argue for a theology of wrath that is imbued with anger, vengeance, and terror, while others, like our friend Bradley Jersak, describe wrath as nothing more than God allowing us to throw a hammer into the air and having it land on our own head.[12] Whatever we say about it, however, the question for us is, "How did Paul mean to use it in Romans 1:18?"

Without giving away the entire plot, let us first warn you that the answer will be so crucial in our understanding of Paul that it will kick off the remainder of this book.

Are you ready for it?

You sure?

Okay, here it is: *not everything Paul writes in Romans is what Paul himself believes*. Remember the Colbert analogy from chapter 1? It comes into play here, especially when considering the so-called "wrath of God." In essence, like much of Romans 1–4 and 9–11, Paul in 1:18–32 is rhetorically and, might we say, sarcastically parroting his theological opponents' views for the sole purpose of crushing their arguments later. Think of it as a bit of a *reductio ad absurdum*, where Paul is cornering his adversaries by their own logic.

IN CLOSING

As we progress further in this book, we will explore these rhetorical techniques, as well as the concept of wrath, in much greater depth, but for now we will leave you with this: just because it says something in the Bible does not mean there is necessarily a "plain reading" of the text. This seems especially true when it comes to the letters of Paul, most notably the epistle to the Romans. Remember, Peter taught us that Paul can be difficult to understand, and that is because he was a master of Greek rhetoric. So, whereas his opponents are playing checkers, Paul is playing chess. Our contention in the chapters that follow, then, is that it was God's plan through Christ to work in Paul to show the world how those who taught (and continue to teach) the false gospel of wrath are, at worst, nothing but liars, but at best, condemned by their own theological premises.

Four

Backdrop to the Apocalyptic View

Before approaching any ancient writing, some of the first questions we must ask ourselves are: *What was the purpose of this text? Why was it written? What goal was the author trying to achieve?* This is called "authorial intent," and though some post-structuralist intellectuals like Jacques Derrida argue that the author's intentions are completely unknowable due to the ever-shifting views of readers, we believe that some form of weak intentionalism[1] should be considered. As Professor of Religion Stanley K. Stowers puts it, "[Our] challenge consists of attempting to imagine how readers in Paul's time might have read the letter while also keeping in view the ways that later Christian communities reshaped it."[2]

When it comes to the letter to the Romans, an overly simplistic answer to the above questions will often go something like this: "Paul was 'called' to preach the good news to the Gentiles,[3] which is why his letters were written to churches with pagan converts in cities like Galatia, Corinth, and Rome." While this is obviously a correct answer (as far as it goes), on its own it lacks contextual depth and fails to address *why* Romans was written *the way it was*. In other words, while Paul's apostleship to the pagans is always in the back of his mind, something very specific was already happening in and around Rome that caused Paul, though he had never set foot there, to take such an interest in the affairs of the church. Moreover, unlike the churches he had founded in Galatia—those who would have known his arguments intimately—his letter to the Romans must flesh out all the philosophical, ethical, and hermeneutical intricacies of his view, given that they would have been novel to many Christians in that city.

With this context in mind, in the sections that follow, we will introduce the main components of the apocalyptic view of Romans, beginning with the villains of this historic drama: *the false teachers* headed to Rome.

THE FALSE TEACHERS

Toward the very end of Romans, Paul makes it abundantly clear why he takes such an interest in the Roman church:

> I urge you, brothers and sisters, to keep an eye on those who create dissensions and hindrances, in opposition to the teaching that you have heard; avoid them. For such people do not serve out Lord Christ but their own appetites, and by smooth talk and flattery they deceive the hearts of the simple-minded (16:17–18).

Mind you, these would have been the very same type of "hostile countermissionaries" Paul angrily refutes in Galatians years prior.[4] Rather than being a blanket exhortation to watch out for generic or speculative false teachers, Paul's words here are pointed and precise. These "gospel of wrath" preachers are not only master manipulators and habitual liars, springing traps and deceiving the "simple-minded" with their "smooth talk," they are on their way to Rome to spread their distorted and corrupted message. In Galatians, he describes these very same kinds of false teachers as those who "pervert" the gospel of Christ,[5] going so far as to wish they would "castrate themselves" for unsettling the church.[6] During his final admonitions in *that* letter, Paul describes the counter-missionaries as blatant hypocrites, writing: "Even the circumcised do not themselves obey the Law, but they want you to be circumcised so that they may boast about your flesh."[7] Again, these are very specific individuals who are attempting to distort the gospel of Christ for their own gain, and they are on their way to Rome, which Paul sees as a dire threat.[8]

For Paul, this "gospel"—which he says is no gospel at all[9]—is an affront to the freedom found in Christ. Remember, he has lived his entire life as a devout Jewish man, and while that never changes, his interpretation of the faith does. Once the scales fall from his eyes,[10] he no longer feels the need to use the Law to lord over others. Eat kosher or don't—*that's not the point*. Keep the Sabbath or don't—*that's not the point*. Become circumcised or don't—*that's not the point*. Eat meat sacrificed to idols or don't—*that's not the point*. But no matter what you do, *do not* force others to do anything that contradicts the freedom one finds in a gospel message devoid of all these cultural and religious rites and markers.

Again, *this* is the context of the first century. Paul's gospel is at risk of being written out of churches he not only founded (Galatia), but those he has not even stepped foot in yet (Rome). And if we know anything about Paul, he is going to see this as an attack and not back down from the fight. That is why his letter to the Galatians is so crass and crude, and why Romans is not much more palatable for those on the other side of his ire.

PAUL'S NONVIOLENT HERMENEUTIC

While Paul is often biting, sarcastic, and perhaps even rude, his hermeneutical approach is decidedly nonviolent. That is to say, the way Paul uses his scriptures is creatively oriented toward peace and nonviolence, rather than wrath and retribution. Whereas traditional Justification Theory seems to pay no mind to this, nor the Damascus Road event that obviously kicks off Paul's peace-oriented transformation, the apocalyptic view of Romans puts it front and center. Throughout this section, we would like to mention two instances where Pauline nonviolence can be found sprinkled in his writings.

Instance 1: Galatians 3:10–13, Referencing Deuteronomy 21:23

In Galatians, Paul is pissed, and for good reason. Like we mentioned above, false teachers in a church he founded are attempting to hijack the gospel and, worse yet, people in that congregation are falling for it. In his own words: "I am astonished that you are so quickly deserting the one who called you in the grace of Christ and are turning to a different gospel."[11]

What is this gospel?

Put most simply, it is "no gospel at all."[12] One reason is that it renders anyone who preaches it a hypocrite. Paul's words to Peter at Antioch sum it up best: "If you, though a Jew, live like a Gentile and not like a Jew, how can you compel the Gentiles to live like Jews?"[13]

Moreover, it is a gospel that forces Christ to take a back seat to a very specific interpretation of "the Law," pitting Gentiles and Jews against each other—as opposed to the truth that both Jews and Gentiles fall short of the glory of God (3:23), yet also under the expansive umbrella of Christ's act of righteousness.[14]

So, what *does* Paul say about works of the Law?

1. It brings a curse.[15]

2. It does not justify anyone before God.[16]

3. It brings wrath (4:15).

4. It brings death (7:9–10; 8:2).

Bottom line: death is where this curse leads—death to even Christ himself. As Paul writes, "Cursed is everyone who is hung on a pole."[17]

The fascinating part about this last statement is that it is a near-direct quote from Deuteronomy 21:23, which reads: "For anyone hung on a tree is under *God's curse*" (emphasis ours). Did you catch the difference in that passage, however? For the writer of the book of Deuteronomy—as well as our Calvinist friends—God's curse is upon anyone who is hung on a tree. But for Paul, such a statement is blasphemy. In fact, in 1 Corinthians 12:3, he clearly states that no one speaking by the spirit of God says "Jesus is cursed," only that he is Lord. Yet, cursed and hanged on a tree is exactly where Jesus ends up anyway—with help from the Law, of course.

What Paul understands about the death of Jesus is clear: God is not the architect of such cursing—God does not create systems that lead to the lynching of his very own son—but rather, an adherence to "works of the Law" is.

Instance 2: Romans 15:7–13, Referencing Various Passages from Psalm 18; Deuteronomy 32:48

Toward the end of Romans, as Paul is concluding his argument that the gospel is for Jews and Gentiles alike—no asterisks needed—he quotes a handful of Old Testament passages to drive the point home. His purpose is to accentuate how Gentiles, "might glorify God for his *mercy*" (15:9, emphasis ours). As he does this, he puts a creative spin on the interpretation, which we will lay out below:

- Keep: Romans 15:9b (quoting Psalm 18:49): "Therefore I will confess you among the Gentiles, and sing praises to your name."

  Delete: Psalm 18:41–42, 46–47: ~~"They cried for help, but there was no one to save them; they cried to the Lord, but he did not answer them. I beat them fine, like dust before the wind; I cast them out like the mire of the streets ... blessed be ... the God who gave me vengeance and subdued peoples under me."~~

- Keep: Romans 15:10 (quoting Deuteronomy 32:43): "And again he says, 'Rejoice, O Gentiles, with his people.'"

  Delete: Last four stanzas of Deuteronomy 32:43: ~~"For he will avenge the blood of his children, and take vengeance on his adversaries, he will repay those who hate him, and cleanse the land for his people."~~

This consistent interpretive pattern is for the sole purpose of eliminating the dividing lines certain Jewish Christians have created in the first century. These teachers falsely taught that an individual must obey the Law—keeping a kosher table, the Sabbath, and enforcing male circumcision—to be under Christ's salvific act. But in Galatians and Romans, Paul is having none of it, because for him, to take away the truth of the gospel with, "laws fabricated in God's absence"[18] is to preach a false gospel—which is no gospel at all.[19]

So, over 10,000 words into this book, and we are finally ready to read Romans in the way it was intended. We have swatted away the need to blend the two soteriological "systems" of Romans 1–4 and 5–8. We have torn down the citadel of Justification Theory, pointing out its many structural flaws along the way. We have set the stage for the drama that would ensue between Paul and the false teachers on their way to Rome. And we have shown how Paul's approach to scripture centers on the peace of God, rather than his supposed retribution. And now, we are finally ready to tackle the epistle the right way.

READING ROMANS RIGHT

In the apocalyptic view of Romans, Paul introduces two systems for how a sinner becomes saved. The first can be thought of as, "works of the Law," while the second emphasizes "faith and trust." Undoubtedly, Paul rejects the first system and accepts the second. Almost no one disagrees with that assessment. But what needs to be brought to the forefront of the conversation is that Justification Theory makes a weird interpretive move whereby it argues for both: phase one sinners must *fail* at the works-based gospel *so that they* can fall into utter despair, thus driving them into phase two, which is the faith-based gospel. What Campbell argues is that this interpretive move is nonsense, and instead, we should make a choice: gospel one or gospel two, not an "oil and water" system that blends both disparate ideas.

Of course, as we noted at the end of the previous chapter, what this means is that not everything written in the letter to the Romans is Paul's personal view. In fact, in many places, the truth is quite the opposite. Often, Paul is quoting his opponents for the purpose of collapsing their arguments in on themselves. As Campbell writes:

> There are certain instances where Paul attributes material to the Teacher directly, using the technique of prosopopoeia. In these texts the Teacher in effect speaks for himself (although suitably crafted by Paul, of course)—first in the opening of his usual conversion speech (1:18–32), and then later in dialogue with Paul (3:1–9). However, for much of the rest of the argument Paul is quoting the Teacher's teaching, and rather sarcastically, and this is entirely consistent with his main rhetorical goal throughout the section, which is to refute the Teacher in terms of his own gospel.[20]

The technique of *prosopop* ... what? What was that word Campbell just used?

Prosopopoeia.

It is simple, really. Prosopopoeia is an ancient rhetorical technique whereby an imagined or absent person or persons are represented as speaking. In the case of Romans, the absent people are the false teachers, and Paul is the one sarcastically representing their argument so that the congregants in

Rome will recognize it when comes out of the mouths of these deceptive counter-missionaries.

So, a difficult word to say (and spell), but a simple concept to understand nonetheless.

Another word we will want to familiarize ourselves with is "diatribe," as it is a key feature of this style of rhetoric. Diatribe can have three distinct flavors:

1. Socratic: Back-and-forth questioning, as seen in Romans 3:1–8.

2. Rhetorical Questioning: i.e., "What shall we say then?"

3. Speech-in-Character: Quoting one's opponent, often sarcastically, in a performative way.

Throughout Romans 1–4, we should notice all these techniques. And when we do, so long as we can divorce ourselves from our presupposed Protestant hermeneutics, the epistle opens for us like pulling curtains to the side of a brilliant, south-facing window. A 30,000-foot reading goes a little something like this:

> Paul kicks off the rhetorical argument with the technique of "speech-in-character" (1:18–32), borrowing heavily from the Jewish propaganda book of Wisdom of Solomon (chapters 13–14 specifically). He does this to get all the Judaizers to nod along in solidarity with the anti-Gentile text. With the false teachers' narrative having the congregants riled up and feeling morally superior, 2:1 then becomes the rhetorical hammer against them. Being even less moral than Gentiles (2:25–29), by their own "works-based gospel" these Judaizers stand condemned. Once they realize this, Paul introduces his gospel, beginning in Romans 5, stating: "Therefore, since we are justified by [the] faith [of Christ], we have peace with God through

our Lord Jesus Christ, through whom we have obtained access to this grace in which we stand, and we boast in our hope of sharing the glory of God" (5:1–2).

That is it! No retribution from above. No hell down below. We are justified by the faithfulness *of* Christ ... full stop. End of paragraph. Drop the mic. Everyone, please drive home safely.

Now, of course we realize that this is just an initial look at the apocalyptic reading of Romans. In the chapters that follow, we will get much more granular, making passage-by-passage comments along the way, so that by the end of Part Three, you will have a firm grasp on all the new concepts we have introduced throughout these first four chapters as well as how they play out in the text itself. So, hang tight and perhaps even grab a Bible. You may want to have it with you as your read the next part of the book.[21]

IN CLOSING

It has taken us damn near half a book to be primed to read the Epistle to the Romans the right way. And by "right" we do not mean right-wing. Nor do we necessarily take a left-wing approach either. What we have attempted to do thus far is meet Paul on his own terms, and though we can never completely distance ourselves from our own subjective reading—presuppositions and all—we believe we have done a fair job of balancing both the author's intent and our own internal biases and subjectivity.

With that, it is now time to get into the text itself. It is time to read Romans right.

PART THREE

A Detailed Exploration of Romans 1–11

"A vast array of difficulties and problems is apparent in its conventional reading, while the rereading offered here, as far as I can tell, resolves all those problems, raising no further difficulties of its own. And this creates a new interpretative state of play."[1]

DOUGLAS A. CAMPBELL
The Deliverance of God

Five

Romans 1:18–32

Wiping the Homophobic Slate Clean

We have finally arrived at the doorstep of reading Romans right, but before we dig too deeply into how the dialogue in Romans 1–4 specifically plays out, let us reiterate how most Protestant commentaries would have us believe that the goal of the early part of the letter is two-fold: to introduce a God of wrath against *all* sinners (1:18) and to attack the evils of one particular sin—*homosexuality* (1:26–27). As we have demonstrated over the course of this book, this view is not only false, but also misses the main point Paul wants to make in this letter, which is:

1. That there are two gospels, Paul's wholly benevolent one (1:16–17) and the false teacher's wrathful one (1:18–32),

2. To follow Christ, you must pick the former over the latter, but...

3. If you fail to do so and instead apply a gospel of "just desserts" to your own life, you will find yourself condemned before *your* wrathful God (2:1).

As it stands, though many Christians will have us believe otherwise, the actual sins listed in 1:18–32 are not all that important; they are just the setup for the rhetorical hammer Paul will throw down, beginning in 2:1 (more on this in the following chapter).

Nevertheless, let us talk about 1:18–32 in this chapter, before turning to Paul's rhetoric in the following one. After his greeting (1:1–13) and introduction of the theme and his gospel (1:14–17), Paul puts forth a highly "Judaized" view of the broader culture the ecclesia[1] in Rome has been immersed in; one the false teachers themselves would have believed and taught. He does this to establish an admittedly skewed cultural context for everything that he will say in the rest of the letter.[2]

But before laying out the specificities of the sins in question, Paul—in the "voice" of those preaching the false gospel—makes it clear that *divine wrath* will be revealed from heaven (1:18) against anyone who has not obeyed (1:21–23), because God has made it plain to all (1:19–20)—Gentiles and Jews alike—exactly what true righteous behavior looks like. "Therefore," he writes:

> God gave them over in the desires of their hearts to impurity, to the dishonoring of their bodies among themselves. They exchanged the truth about God for a lie and worshiped and served the creature rather than the Creator [...] For this reason, God gave them over to dishonorable passions. Their females exchanged natural intercourse for unnatural, and in the same way also the males, giving up natural intercourse with females, were consumed with their passionate desires for one another. Males committed shameless acts with males and received in their own persons the due penalty for their error. And since they did not see fit to acknowledge God, God gave them over to an unfit mind and to do things that should not be done (1:24–28).

Because of Christianity's fascination with condemning the LGBTQ+ community, allow us say that there is no reason to believe that what is being described here is—no matter whose "voice" it comes from—analogous to what we would today refer to as homosexuality.[3] There are plenty of others who agree with us on this, too. For example, Aristides, a first-century church father, as well as second-century Christian apologist, Justin Martyr, offer the following assessments. First, Aristides, who lived just seventy years after Paul, uses nearly the same language as the apostle, saying how Gentiles engaged in *idolatry* and *sexual worship of false gods*, writing:

> The Barbarians, then, as they did not apprehend God, went astray among the elements, and began to worship things created instead of their Creator; and for this end they made images and shut them up in shrines.[4]

In the second century, Justin Martyr also affirms this historical context when he writes:

> But as for us, we have been taught that to expose newly-born children is the part of wicked men; and this we have been taught lest we should do any one an injury, and lest we should sin against God, first, because we see that almost all so exposed (not only the girls, but also the males) are brought up to prostitution. And as the ancients are said to have reared herds of oxen, or goats, or sheep, or grazing horses, so now we see you rear children only for this shameful use; and for this pollution a multitude of females and hermaphrodites, and those who commit unmentionable iniquities, are found in every nation. And you receive the hire of these, and duty and taxes from them, whom you ought to exterminate from your realm. And any one who uses such persons, besides the godless and infamous and impure intercourse, may possibly be having intercourse with his own child, or relative, or brother. And there are some who prostitute even their own children and wives, and some are openly mutilated for the purpose of sodomy; and they refer these mysteries to the mother of the

> gods, and along with each of those whom you esteem gods there is painted a serpent, a great symbol and mystery. Indeed, the things which you do openly and with applause, as if the divine light were overturned and extinguished, these you lay to our charge; which, in truth, does no harm to us who shrink from doing any such things, but only to those who do them and bear false witness against us.[5]

These are not exactly "progressive" Christian sources, nor are they the only ones who agree with us on the matter. Renowned biblical scholar Matthew Henry, Scottish evangelist Robert Haldane, and Reformed Presbyterian Charles Hodge all argue that what the author is referring to in Romans 1 is a condemnation of pagan sexual temple practices of prostitution. First, here's Henry:

> In Isaiah's time it [idolatry] abounded, witness the abominable idolatries of Ahaz (which some think are particularly referred to here—Isaiah 57) and of Manasseh. They were dotingly fond of their idols, were inflamed with them, as those that burn in unlawful unnatural lusts (Romans 1:27). They were mad upon their idols (Jeremiah 50:38). They inflamed themselves with them by their violent passions in the worship of them, as those of Baal's prophets that leaped upon the altar, and cut themselves (1 Kings 18:26,28). Justly therefore were they given up to their own hearts' lusts.[6]

Haldane offers a similar interpretation:

> The Apostle having awfully depicted the magnitude of Pagan wickedness, and having shown that their ungodliness in aban-

> doning the worship of the true God was the reason why they had been abandoned to their lusts, here descends into particulars, for the purpose of showing to what horrible excesses God had permitted them to proceed. This was necessary, to prove how odious in the sight of God is the crime of idolatry. Its recompense was this fearful abandonment. It was also necessary, in order to give a just idea of human corruption, as evinced in its monstrous enormities when allowed to take its course, and also in order to exhibit to believers a living proof of the depth of the evil from which God had delivered them; and, finally, to prove the falsity of the Pagan religion since, so far from preventing such excesses, it even incited and conducted men to their commission.[7]

Finally, Hodge agrees with them both, arguing:

> The reasons why Paul refers in the first instance to the sins of uncleanness, in illustration and proof of the degradation of the heathen, probably were, that those sins are always intimately connected with idolatry, forming at times even a part of the service rendered to the false gods.[8]

If you doubt our assessment, we invite you to go back and reread Romans 1 from the very beginning. Even if you are yet to be convinced that 1:18–32 is in the "voice" of Paul's opponents—we will get to *that* in the following chapter—what you will observe is a progression in the argumentation that begins with a condemnation of pagan idol worship and ends with a description of what that worship involves and how God punishes those who engage in the practice.

For example, starting in 1:18, the author's admonishment reads as follows: "The wrath of God is being revealed from heaven against all the godlessness and wickedness of people, who suppress the truth by their wickedness." Who is the author referring to here? Very clearly, the passage is about the "godless" and "wicked" people in general. In 1:21, of these folks' thinking, it is said that they, "became futile and their foolish hearts were darkened." Then, it is asserted how they, "claimed to be wise but became fools" (1:22), and in 1:23 that they, "exchanged the glory of the immortal God for images made to look like a mortal human being and birds and animals and reptiles."

All told, this is the very definition of idol worship, not "homosexuality." Let us all agree on that much. According to the text, these wicked and godless people denied the knowledge of God and began to worship idols. Because of this, "God gave them over in the sinful desires of their hearts to sexual impurity for the degrading of their bodies with one another." (1:24)

Again, for sake of argument, allow us to reiterate and say that *even if* 1:18–32 is the "voice" of Paul rather than that of the false teachers—it is *not*, but bear with us—the message here is clear: what is being condemned is the use of sexual intercourse as part of the worship of created things, or, in other words, *idols*.

At the end of the day, it can be argued that lust is lust. In a first-century context, ritual pagan sex qualifies as, "degrading their bodies with one another"—whether gay or straight. The passage goes on, continuing its progressive thought in 1:26: "For this reason God gave them over to dishonorable passions."

Because of *what* reason?

It is because these people—who were engaged in worshipping pagan idols—started degrading their bodies with one another in ritual sexual intercourse (most likely devoid of consent), so "God gave them over to shameful lusts." And so, it must be said that what is being described here would be immoral in the eyes of first-century Roman Christians no matter if the sex were gay *or* straight. Can you see that? If we were to reread those verses above and substitute heterosexual intercourse into the text, the point would still be the same. Why? Because the focus of the argument is that these pagan worship practices are what is evil—not the "gayness" of the sexual intercourse the people are engaging in.[9]

After the teacher's statement in 1:26a, he continues:

> Even their women exchanged natural sexual relations for unnatural ones. In the same way, the men also abandoned natural relations with women and were inflamed with lust for one another. Men committed shameful acts with other men, and received in themselves the due penalty for their error.

Keep in mind that what is being said here is that anyone who is "inflamed with lust" is in sin—whether gay, straight, or otherwise.[10] The entire flow of thought begins with a discussion about those who deny God, worship created things rather than the creator, engage in ritualistic sexual intercourse as part of that worship, and then—because of all these things—are judged by God and given over to their lusts.

So, let us ask you *this*: What if the teacher's descriptions here went as follows:

1. People denied God
2. Those people worshipped idols
3. They worshipped idols by engaging in *heterosexual* intercourse

Would you conclude that God hated heterosexual intercourse in general, or a particular "brand" of heterosexuality, one in the context of "denying God and worshipping idols?"

We hope you can see how the latter is a more accurate reply, but too often Christians opt for the out-of-context former response to condemn "homosexual intercourse" as such. But if we do not read Romans 1 as a de facto condemnation of straight sex—and most of the chapter *is* about so-called straight sex—then why do we read it as a condemnation of gay sexual activity? Could it be because some have a bias against gay sex that they do not have against straight sex?

If we lay aside our inherent bias against gay sex, we can see that the entire point of 1:18–32 is that the denial of God and the worship of idols through sexual intercourse is what is seen as "shameful." Sexual intercourse performed in the worship of idols is what is being critiqued here. That is the entire point of this rhetorical argument. Straight sex is not evil. Gay sex is not evil. What matters is the context. Does the sexual intercourse involve two people who love one another? Do they happen to also love and trust in God? If so, then this type of sex is not being spoken about in Romans 1.

As we close, we hope that you, our readers, will continue to keep an open mind about what we have been discussing in this chapter. Yes, there are queer Christians; yes, they are wonderful; and no, the "wrath of God" is not coming for them. As we will discover in 2:5, the only wrath that is coming for anyone is the wrath stored up by ourselves by our hard and impenitent hearts—that is, any time we judge others for the "sins" of 1:18–32 while doing the very same thing behind closed doors. *To suggest otherwise* is the abomination, not the lives of our LGBTQ+ brothers and sisters. Instead, they are often the epitome of what it means to be Christ followers, displaying an exceptional capacity for grace and Christlike love for the very people who shun and marginalize them. The irony, of course, is that too often Christians will use Romans 1:18–32 to condemn these same people, never realizing how they are playing the role of the False Teacher. In the following chapter, we will show you exactly how this is the case.

Six

Romans 2

Paul's Rhetorical Chess Move

Prior to diving headlong into Paul's rhetorical shift in 2:1, it is probably a good idea to stop and point out something very significant to our conversation about how to read Romans right. When we approach this epistle—or any book of the Bible, for that matter—we must understand that, in its original form, there were no chapters or verses. Such demarcations were added much later by those who wanted to make it easier to refer to a specific section of the text.

This is noteworthy because, quite often, the now common delineations do violence to the message itself. For example, whenever we as readers begin a new chapter, we tend to approach it as if what we are reading is a brand-new idea or thought that the author wants to emphasize *apart* from what has just come before; but often, the reverse is true. As we have demonstrated, when it comes to Paul's letter thus far, all the juicy rhetoric we have just read in 1:18- 32 is the very set-up to the hammer that is Romans 2. It is the continuation of a single thought or line of dialogue and *not* a pivot to a brand-new idea.

Another example of when a chapter break prevents us from noticing the context of a passage is found in Luke 21. After Jesus is seen looking up to witness the rich putting their offerings into the treasury in the Temple, he famously points to the poor widow and says, "[She] has put in more than all; for all these out of their abundance have put in offerings for God, but she out of her poverty put in all the livelihood that she had."[1]

Most evangelical-leaning teachers of the Bible will point to this verse as an example of how Jesus honors those who "give all that they have" to the church. But they miss his entire point because they fail to connect this scene with the ending of the previous chapter, which says:

> Beware of the scribes, who desire to go around in long robes, love greetings in the marketplaces, the best seats in the synagogues, and the best places at feasts, *who devour widows' houses*, and for a pretense make long prayers. These will receive greater condemnation.[2]

Without the chapter break between the end of Luke 20 and the beginning of Luke 21, we can more easily see that what Jesus says about the poor widow is in the context of condemning the scribes who "devour widows' houses" by demanding tithes from them without showing mercy. In this new context, Jesus' words about the widow's mite are anything but warm and fuzzy praises for those who "give all that they have" to the church. Rather, they are an indictment of the religious leaders who take all they can from the poorest among them without concern for their needs.

With this knowledge in mind, let us try to approach what Paul says in Romans 2 as a continuation of everything he has said in 1:18–32. Remember, he has just spent an entire chapter railing against "those filthy pagans" who do abominable sexual things in their worship of false pagan deities. His entire plan here is to get his readers riled up about "those Gentile sinners over there" who do not follow the Law of God, and who do not believe in Jesus as the Messiah. Simply put, everything up to this point has been a rhetorical setup for what is about to happen in 2:1, where Paul writes:

> *Therefore, you are without excuse, whoever you are, when you judge others, for in passing judgment on another you condemn yourself, because you, the judge, are doing the very same things.*

> *We know that God's judgment on those who do such things is in accordance with truth. Do you imagine, whoever you are, that when you judge those who do such things and yet do them yourself, you will escape the judgment of God* (2:1–3)?

Take that, *whoever you are*!

Paul turns the tables on his readers by baiting them into a frenzy of righteous indignation against those "filthy pagans" who do detestable things and then essentially asks, "Are you judging those pagans right now? I guess that means you are without sin. If not, then you have just exposed your hypocrisy as a sinner, too." This is like Jesus saying, "let the one without sin cast the first stone"[3] to the men who accuse the woman caught in adultery; or, when the Lord says, "take the log out of your own eye before you try to take the speck out of your brother's eye."[4]

Paul sets the trap and the false-teaching Christians in Rome have fallen right into it.[5] That is to say, Romans 2 is the punchline to the Romans 1:18–32 set-up. He starts by "pretending" to stand with those who pass judgment on others who commit sinful acts, and then turns and says, "Wait a minute, are you judging those people as unrighteous sinners? You are guilty, too—by your own logic!"

It is a brilliant way of catching his readers off guard and establishing the idea that they need to take a step back before rushing to judgment. In other words, as he universalizes the false teacher's application of "just desserts," the hope is that they would learn some humility before going any further.

But that is not the entirety of the situation going on in the first part of this epistle. It is not as simple as, "approach your faith with humility, lest you become a hypocrite," *whoever you are*. As we discussed in chapter 4, the Roman church is at a crossroads and Paul is theologically standing toe to toe with savvy false teachers on their way to the city, so a large segment of this letter is rhetorically written using a common argumentation device from the first century known as *prosopopoeia*. If you recall, prosopopoeia is when an author attempts to prove a point by writing in the style of those who would disagree with them *so that they* can refute those arguments in their own voice. Think of it as a debate where one person handles both sides of the argument.

We can see this argumentative style initiated early in the letter, where Paul's own view—let us call it the voice of the Gospel Teacher—says one thing while his opponent—let us call it the voice of the False Teacher—counters his view. Below, we have emphasized Paul in italics and the false gospel in bold:

> *For I am not ashamed of the Gospel; it is the power of God for salvation to everyone who has faith (or trusts in God). To the Jew first, and also to the Greek. For in this God's justice is revealed, out of faithfulness into faithfulness. As it is written, "And the upright shall live by faithfulness"* (1:16–17, DBH).
>
> **For God's vehemence against all the impiety and injustice of human beings, who by injustice suppress the truth, is revealed from heaven, because what is known of God is manifest among them, because God made it manifest to them** (1:18–19, DBH).

Here, we have two voices speaking: one is the voice that Paul himself was trained as a Pharisee to speak from, and the other voice is the one that the risen Christ taught him to speak from. For those who enjoy historical inaccuracies, this is Saul versus Paul, if you will—the teacher of the Law versus the teacher of the Gospel.

One way to notice the two different voices is that, in the early part of our example above, Paul says that, "God's *justice* is revealed..." while later, the voice of the False Teacher responds by saying, "God's *vengeance* [or wrath] is revealed..." While Justification Theory may conflate these two concepts—justice and wrath—Paul wants to emphasize the *distinction* by demonstrating that the unveiling of God's justice is done through the person of Jesus Christ, while the False Teacher tends to emphasize God's wrath upon those who fail to keep the *Law*.

Incidentally, this back and forth is only the beginning, as we will continue to witness such rhetoric all throughout the first four chapters of the epistle, as well as throughout Romans 9–11—one voice speaking of God's justice as revealed in Christ, and the other appealing to God's wrath; one point of view says that salvation is about trusting (or having faith) in God's work on our behalf, and the other is that salvation is about faithfulness to observing holiness codes and following the Mosaic Law.

Now, before we go much further in our discussion of the two voices, it is worth noting the similarities between the False Teacher and folks like Peter and James. If you recall what happens in chapter 15 of the book of Acts, Paul confronts Peter for wanting to Judaize the Gentile believers and even separates himself from those same people whenever James and other Jewish Christians happen to be around. Paul's harsh and quite public rebuke of Peter and any other Jewish Christian leader who imposed Mosaic Law upon Gentile believers is strong evidence that this practice was a problem in the early church. Furthermore, since Paul did not personally establish the churches in Rome, it is quite likely that those who did were following more closely to the Judaizers like Peter and James than they were the more liberating teachings of Paul, and would have therefore welcomed the gospel of the False Teacher on its way there.[6]

The tension in question is between the gospel of grace taught by Paul and the false gospel of Torah adherence taught by Peter, James, and others who argued that one must first take on Jewish markers before following Jesus.[7] Incidentally, this is the exact same tension found here in Romans between Paul and the False Teacher.

Getting back to our exploration of the rhetoric found in Romans 2, let us look at a few more examples of these two voices. We have already established that the False Teacher begins their argument back in 1:18, with it running all the way through the end of the chapter. This is their rhetorical opening, and is "the fullest presentation of the Teacher's position that we receive from the hand of Paul."[8] Romans 2 is where the voice of Paul responds to the condemnation of the False Teacher, his rhetoric being most biting right before hitting them with yet another punchline, *"So by your hard and impenitent heart you are storing up wrath for yourself on the day of wrath, when God's righteous judgment will be revealed"* (2:5). Notice, however, where the wrath comes from: *you!* Paul mentions it three times—by *your* hard heart *you* store up wrath for *yourself*. It is not God who brings wrath, says Paul; it is *you* (whoever you are!).

Paul then again quotes the false teacher:

> **He will repay according to each one's deeds: to those who by patiently doing good seek for glory and honor and immortality, he will give eternal life, while for those who are self-seeking and who obey not the truth but injustice, there will be wrath and fury** (2:6–8).

The False Teacher cannot help but return to the *quid pro quo* version of God and continually emphasizes how God's "wrath and fury" will come down on those who fail to "do good." We are again back in the realm of "just desserts." In contrast, Paul's assertion is that what is truly revealed is God's true justice as manifest through the love and life of Christ (5:1).

Nevertheless, the False Teacher continues:

> **There will be affliction and distress for everyone who does evil, both the Jew first and the Greek, but glory and honor and peace for everyone who does good, both the Jew first and the Greek. For God shows no partiality** (2:9–11).

Here, the False Teacher concedes that all who do evil—both Jews and Gentiles—will experience distress and anguish, and, thinking they are justified in such a view, boasts how "God shows no partiality." Finally, the false teacher concludes:

> **All who have sinned apart from the law will also perish apart from the law, and all who have sinned under the law will be judged in accordance with the law. For it is not the hearers of the law who are righteous in God's sight but the doers of the law who will be justified** (2:12–13).

Notice that, according to the False Teacher, it is the Law that is the measuring stick for what is righteous and upright. For Paul, however, this does not fit within his gospel, so he makes the following devastating point:

> *When gentiles, who do not possess the law, by nature do what the law requires, these, though not having the law, are a law to themselves. They show that what the law requires is written on their hearts, as their own conscience also bears witness, and their conflicting thoughts will accuse or perhaps excuse them on the day when, according to my gospel, God through Christ Jesus judges the secret thoughts of all* (2:14–16).

Paul's point against the False Teacher is that Gentiles keep the Law without knowing it, and that this instinct to do good proves that God has written his Law upon their hearts, void of any Torah-derived rites and markers.

The following section is where Paul really pours it on. Starting in 2:17 and continuing to 2:29, the apostle makes the very strong case that this teacher of the Law and others like him are causing *"God's name* [to be] *blasphemed among the Gentiles"* (2:24) because they teach others to keep the Law that they themselves cannot keep. Paul's universalizing argument culminates in this point, which concludes Romans 2:

> *For a person is not a Jew who is one outwardly, nor is circumcision something external and physical. Rather, a person is a Jew who is one inwardly, and circumcision is a matter of the heart, by the Spirit, not the written code. Such a person receives praise not from humans but from God* (2:28–29).

Here, Paul's argument is that what makes someone a Jew—and by this he means a member of those who are the "chosen" people of God—is not determined by anything outward. That includes not only circumcision among men but even the racial identity as one who is born Jewish. Instead, what makes someone a child of Abraham has more to do with what is going on in their heart. So, this is a "spiritual and not physical" reality, says the apostle.

Paul makes this very same argument in his letter to the Galatians when he writes:

> Understand, then, that those who have faith are children of Abraham [...] So in Christ Jesus you are all children of God through faith [...] If you belong to Christ, then you are Abraham's seed, and heirs according to the promise.[9]

Those who are in Christ are the true Children of Abraham, Paul says. It has nothing to do with who your parents are, or whether you keep the Law of Moses or not. It has everything to do with being in Christ. Full stop.

So, who are the ones who are in Christ? Is this only those who pray the prayer and join the church? Paul responds to that question a little later, so let us put a pin in it until he does. For now, allow us to continue to follow the back-and-forth debate between Paul and the False Teacher as it carries on into Romans 3.

Seven

ROMANS 3–4

Diatribe and Closing Arguments

THE FIRST QUESTION PAUL asks the False Teacher after laying out his argument in 2:14–29 is this: *"Then what advantage has the Jew? Or what is the value of circumcision?"* (3:1) Undoubtedly, this is an obvious inquiry, given Paul's disregard for either classification—circumcised or uncircumcised—as it pertains to salvation. What Paul is ultimately wanting to do is spring another trap on the False Teacher, this time by making his opponent apply their own logic of a retributive God to themselves. Here is how the teacher initially responds: **"Much, in every way! For in the first place, the Jews were entrusted with the oracles of God"** (3:2).

Paul, knowing he has just gotten his opponent to admit an advantage, then follows up: *"What then? If some were unfaithful, will their infidelity annul God's fidelity?"* (3:3, DBH).

To which the Teacher responds, **"Let it not be so! But let God be truthful and every man a liar, as has been written, 'So that you might be vindicated in your words and may prevail when you are judged'"** (3:4, DBH).

Paul again jumps in: *"And if our injustice serves to exhibit God's justice, what shall we say? That the God who enforces this indignation is unjust?"* (3:5, DBH).

To which the Teacher says: **"Let it not be so! Else how will God judge the cosmos?"** (3:6, DBH).

Once again, Paul retorts, *"Yet, if through my falsehood God's truth overflowed to his glory, why am I still also judged as a sinner?"* (3:7, DBH).

To which the Teacher responds: **"And why not (as we are slandered and as some claim we teach): 'Let us do evil things that good things may come?' Their condemnation is deserved!"** (3:8).

Knowing that he has now essentially gotten the teacher to contradictorily admit there is *no* advantage to being a Jew, Paul again asks: *"What then? Are we any better off?"* (3:9a).

"No, not at all," the Teacher admits.

Paul has ensnared him. The False Teacher has just contradicted himself. Paul then goes for the jugular to prove that Jews have no eschatological advantage over Gentiles:

> *For we have already charged that both Jew and Gentile are under the power of sin. As it is written: "There is no one who is righteous, not even one; there is no one who has understanding, there is no one who seeks God. All have turned aside, together they have become worthless; there is no one who shows kindness, there is not even one. Their throats are opened graves; they use their tongues to deceive. The venom of vipers is under their lips. Their mouths are full of cursing and bitterness. Their feet are swift to shed blood; ruin and misery are in their paths, and the way of peace they have not known. There is no fear of God before their eyes"* (3:9b–18).

Do you see the back-and-forth dialogue and what Paul is attempting to do? Is it not quite clear that there are two voices here? Each one has their own perspective and, though Paul is dictating—often sarcastically—where the conversation goes, on the surface it appears as if two people are openly and honestly reasoning together over the differences between Jews and Gentiles and what makes either of them righteous or unrighteous in the eyes of God. Paul has one clear perspective and the False Teacher has another.

In all actuality, as we stated earlier, Paul is setting a trap. The apostle makes the case, using the answers of the False Teacher, that both Jews and Gentiles are unrighteous in God's eyes, regardless of whether they "keep the Law," and furthermore, that no one even keeps the Law anyway. All have sinned. God is no respecter of persons. The difference, then, is that under the False Teacher's system, all are utterly condemned. In Campbell's words: "Paul elicits in this manner from the mouth of the interlocutor—here doubtless representing the Teacher directly—the unequivocal condemnation of *anyone* who is sinful. No rejoinders or excuses are accepted by the Teacher in 3:1–9a, as he sternly defends the justice of God."[1] Hence, the Teacher is royally screwed by his own logic.

So, what is the solution, according to Paul?

It is quite simple, he says: the Justification of God, which is given freely to everyone—both the Jew and the Gentile—is handed out regardless of whether they observe the Law or not. This is why he begins to tease out his gospel, writing:

> *But now, God's justice has been manifested apart from the Law, being attested by the Law and the prophets, and, by the faithfulness of Jesus the Anointed, God's justice is for everyone. For there is no distinction since all have sinned and fall short of the glory of God, they are now justified by his gift of grace through the redemption that is in Christ Jesus* (3:21–24, DBH).

Paul's words here introduce the radical idea that justification, righteousness, and forgiveness are all given freely to everyone by God, irrespective of the Law and apart from sacrifices. This is the main point of Paul's letter: It is by the faithfulness *of* Christ—and nothing more—that *everyone* is justified. This is why Paul goes on to say the following:

> [Jesus Christ was] *put forward* [by God] *on account of faithfulness as a conciliation* [expiation] *in his blood as a demonstration of his justice through the dismissal of past sins in God's mercy—for the demonstration of his justice in the present season—that he might be just and that the one vindicated might be made so from the faithfulness of Jesus* (3:25–26, DBH).

Of this passage, Girardian New Testament scholar Robert Hamerton-Kelly remarks:

> Clearly, we are on the way to a radical reorientation of the understanding of the relationship between the death of Christ and the sacrificial categories of Judaism, which entails a restatement of the sense in which Christ's death can be called a sacrifice. The major new element is that Paul inverts the traditional understanding of sacrifice so that God is the offerer, not the receiver, and the scapegoat goes into the sacred (community) rather than out of it.[2]

Paul's radical reorientation does not go unnoticed and the reaction by the False Teacher is swift.

"Then what becomes of boasting?" he asks.

"It is excluded," Paul says.

"By what law? By that of works?" the False Teacher asks.

"No," says Paul, *"but by the law of faith. For we hold that a person is justified by faith (trusting in Christ) apart from the works prescribed by the Law."*

The False Teacher retorts, **"Or, is God the God of the Jews only?"**

To which Paul responds, *"Is he not the God of the Gentiles also?"*

"Yes," says the False Teacher, **"of the Gentiles also."**

Paul interjects, *"since God is one, he will justify the circumcised on the grounds of faith, and the uncircumcised through that same faith."*

The False Teacher then asks, **"Do we now throw out the Law by this faith?"**

To which Paul responds, *"By no means! On the contrary, we uphold the Law."*

The conversation continues into Romans 4, with the False Teacher asking: **"What then are we to say was gained by Abraham, our ancestor according to the flesh? For if Abraham was justified by works, he has something to boast about..."** to which Paul interjects, *"...but not before God. For what does the scripture say? 'Abraham believed God, and it was reckoned to him as righteousness'"* (4:1–3).

With that, the False Teacher is silenced until we hear from them again in Romans 9.

Without a doubt, once you see the speech-in-character approach to Romans you cannot unsee it, and seeing it reveals that the voice of Paul is the voice arguing for God's unmerited favor and endless mercy for everyone, regardless of their outward perceived righteousness. That, for him, *is* the gospel. Pitted against him—as it was in Galatia and Jerusalem—are teachers who bring a false gospel of wrath and condemnation, and Paul wants the hearers of his letters to know which one to choose.

Throughout the remainder of Romans 4, Paul continues to make his point about the difference between working for something and receiving something as a gift. If Abraham—and by association *all* other Jewish people—was justified by keeping the Law, then it does not make sense to say that God attributed righteousness to Abraham *freely*. Either Abraham was owed that by God in return for his works, or it was freely given to Abraham because of his simple trust in God alone. Or, as Paul puts it: *"Now to one who works, wages are not reckoned as a gift but as something due. But to one who without works trusts him who justifies the ungodly, such faith is reckoned as righteousness"* (4:4-5).

This is an idea that he wants to further develop in this chapter, as he continues:

> *Is this blessedness, then, pronounced only on the circumcised, or also on the uncircumcised? We say, "Faith was reckoned to Abraham as righteousness." How then was it reckoned to him? Was it before or after he had been circumcised? It was not after, but before he was circumcised. He received the sign of circumcision as a seal of the righteousness that he had by faith while he was still uncircumcised. The purpose was to make him the ancestor of all who believe without being circumcised and who thus have righteousness reckoned to them...* (4:9–11, DBH).

The words penned above mark an enormous point in Paul's argument that keeping the Law has nothing to do with being righteous in the eyes of God. If Abraham was counted as righteous by God *after* he was circumcised, then the False Teacher could claim that his righteousness was conditional upon keeping the Law. But that is not the case. Therefore, Paul argues, God does not measure righteousness according to obedience to the Mosaic Law, and furthermore, that Abraham was made, *"the ancestor of all who believe without being circumcised and who (also) have righteousness reckoned to them."*

Before giving his opponent any opening, Paul quickly adds:

> *If it is the adherents of the law who are to be the heirs, faith is null and the promise is void* [...] *For this reason, it depends on faith, in order that the promise may rest on grace and be guaranteed to all his descendants, not only to the adherents of the law*

> *but also to those who share the faith of Abraham (for he is the father of all of us)* (4:14, 16).

After juxtaposing the Law and faith, Paul, who is nearly complete in his dismantling of the False Teacher's arguments, concludes:

> *Therefore his faith "was reckoned to him as righteousness." Now the words, "it was reckoned to him," were written not for his sake alone, but for ours also. It will be reckoned to us who believe in him who raised Jesus our Lord from the dead, who was handed over to death for our trespasses and was raised for our justification* (4:22–25).

Notice the pattern here: Faith leads to righteousness, not primarily for the one who has faith, but for "ours also." It is all about *us*! It is a gift freely given despite "our trespasses." It is a raising to life for "our justification." Everything is for us devoid of any of the *quid pro quo* language of Justification Theory.

Though this is the end of Romans 4, it is only the beginning of Paul's gospel, which runs from Romans 5 through 8. In the next chapter, we will cover it all, before turning to one final confrontation with the False Teacher in 9–11. Are you ready? Let us get into it then!

Eight

Romans 5–8

The Apocalyptic Gospel of Paul

UNPACKING THE GOSPEL IN CHAPTER 5

Finally, we arrive at Paul's fully fleshed-out, wholly benevolent gospel, where he begins by boldly asserting that we all have been vindicated (or rectified) by the faithfulness *of* Christ (cf. 3:22) and that we all have peace with God because of what Jesus accomplished in both his death and resurrection (5:1–2). Moreover, as Campbell notes, participation in Christ's death and resurrection is available to all who trust in Christ's faith, which liberates all from the Law.[1] For Paul, the heart of the gospel is this:

> God shows his own love to us in that, *while we were yet sinners*, the Anointed [Christ] died on our behalf. So much more, therefore, shall we—having now been vindicated [rectified] by *his* blood—be saved from the indignation. For if, being enemies, we were reconciled with God through his Son's death, *so much the more* shall we—having been reconciled—be saved through his life—though not only that: rather boasting also in God through our Lord Jesus the Anointed, through whom we have *received* reconciliation (5:8–11, DBH, our emphasis).

Two points need to be made here:

1. This passage is emblematic of what we have meant all along by an "apocalyptic" gospel. The Greek word simply means "an unveiling." What once was secret now has been made known—that God shows his love and mercy to his enemies, even those who have murdered his son, extending his salvation to everyone, not merely those who are obedient to his commands.

2. There is only one thing to boast in: God through Christ. In other words, we boast in the faithfulness *of* God, not our own faith. We have *received* reconciliation, so "trust it to be true," says Paul.

It is at this point in the letter where we arrive at the juxtaposition of Adam and Christ, and where Augustine's pernicious doctrine of original sin finds its genesis. At the heart of this monstrous Protestant staple is 5:12, a text New Testament scholar David Bentley Hart has referred to as, "one of the most consequential mistranslations in Christian history."[2] Most modern English translations render the text something like the following: "Therefore, just as sin came into the world through one man, and death through sin, and so death spread to all men because all sinned" (ESV).

We are all familiar with this passage, but where does a translation like this go wrong? Hart explains:

> [The] notoriously defective rendering (of this verse) in the Latin Vulgate [...] became the standard reading of the verse in much of Western theology after the late fourth century: "in whom (i.e. Adam) all sinned." This is the locus classicus of the Western Christian notion of original guilt (or original sin)—the idea that in some sense all human beings had sinned in Adam, and that therefore everyone is born already damnably guilty in the eyes of God—a logical and moral para-

> dox that Easter tradition was spared by its reliance on the original Greek.[3]

While the doctrine of original sin may line up with Justification Theory—that all are damnably guilty in the eyes of a retributive God—it does not fit with the thrust of Paul's arguments as we have understood them throughout this book. As the apostle explains, sin, which he describes as both a disease and enslavement to an unjust master, is never to be understood as, "an inherited condition of criminal culpability,"[4] but instead that the, "disease of death and the contagion of sin" are intimately connected, and that, "just as sin entered into the cosmos and introduced death into all its members, so the contagion of death spread into the whole of humanity and introduced sin into all its members. This [...] is for Paul the very dynamism of death and sin that is reversed in Christ: by his triumphant righteousness he introduced eternal life into the cosmos, and so as that life spreads into the whole of humanity it makes all righteous."[5]

In other words, sin and death are inextricably linked *so that they* can be utterly destroyed by the righteousness and life found in Christ. Paul begins the unraveling process in 5:15: "For if by the transgression of the one the many died, so much the more did God's grace and the gift in grace of the one man, Jesus the Anointed, overflow to the many" (DBH). In 5:17–19, Paul continues:

> For if, by the one's transgression (Adam) death reigned through the one, so much more will those receiving grace's abundance and the gift of righteousness reign in life through the one Jesus the Anointed—so, then just as by one transgression unto condemnation for all human beings, so also by one act of righteousness unto rectification of life for all human beings; for just as by the heedlessness of the one man the many

> were rendered sinners, so also by the obedience of the one the many will be rendered upright (or righteous) (DBH).

The same universalizing idea is also present in parallel verses found in 1 Corinthians 14:21–22, where Paul boldly proclaims: "For, since through a man (Adam) death, then through a man (Jesus) resurrection from the dead. For just as in Adam all die, so also in the Anointed all will be given life" (DBH).

In other words, just as the first sin of Adam brought condemnation and death to absolutely everyone in the way the worst type of contagion might affect absolutely everyone in a global pandemic,[6] so, too, did Christ's final act of righteousness bring eternal life and rectification to absolutely everyone, bar none.

Now, as we have noted, sin and death are inextricably linked to Adam, and are contrasted by the faithfulness and righteousness of Christ. In a similar fashion, Paul ends chapter 5 by making yet another juxtaposition, this time between the Law and grace, writing:

> The Law was introduced in order that transgression might abound; and where sin was abundant, Grace was superabundant, in order that, as sin reigned in death, so also Grace might now reign through uprightness for life in the Age to come through Jesus the Anointed (5:20–21, DBH, our paraphrase).

What Paul is saying here is simple, and reiterates his earlier point that whatever happens because of sin—including a knowledge of its increase derived *from* the Law—is undone because of Christ's faithful act of righteousness.

EXPOUNDING ON PARTICIPATION IN CHAPTER 6

Having made his main point in Romans 5, Paul continues to expand on his argument that all have been made righteous in Christ—even those who are the enemies of God—by asking a series of rhetorical questions about our participation in such an event: "What shall we say then? Should we persist in sin so that grace might abound?" (These are the same types of questions posed in 3:8, during the diatribe between Paul and the False Teacher.) The answer, as before, is "Let it not be! We who have died to sin, how shall we still live in it? Or are you unaware that we—as many as were baptized into the Anointed One, Jesus—were baptized into his death?" (6:2–3).

Here, Paul continues to press the idea that what was done to Christ and what Christ has accomplished is credited to all of us, in the same way that Adam's sin was accounted to us under the Law. So, if Christ has died, we have died with him. If Christ has been raised, we have also been raised to new life. If Christ is seated at the right-hand of the Father, then we are also seated there with Christ (6:4).[7] Again, such sentiment echoes something we said at the beginning of the chapter, which is that in Paul's view of the gospel, Christ's death and resurrection is something anyone can participate in. Just have trust that Christ's faith will carry you through (regardless of *your* potential lack of faith).

To reiterate the point, Paul begins to answer the rhetorical questions posed at the beginning of Romans 6:

> So also we reckon ourselves to be dead to sin, yet also living for God in the Anointed One, Jesus. So do not let sin reign in [your] mortal body, for the purpose of obeying its lusts; neither present your bodily members to sin as weapons of iniquity; rather, present yourselves to God as those alive from

> the dead, and your bodily members to God as weapons of uprightness, for sin shall not dominate, for you are not under the Law, but rather under Grace (6:11–14, DBH).

In other words, since we have once died to sin and been raised to new life with Christ, we are yet still dead to sin and yet still alive in Christ—by God's grace. Even so, when we *were* "slaves to sin," God's grace abounded even more, so as to liberate all "from sin [and into enslavement] to righteousness" (6:16–18). But now that we have experienced this marvelous grace of God, we are free from the power of sin over our lives and free to live the new life of Christ in the kingdom reality that has now come.

At this point, some might inevitably ask, what about the Law Paul previously said should not be disregarded? What are we to make of it now that we are under the power of God's unending grace? That is exactly what Paul wants to explain next.

REFRAMING THE LAW IN CHAPTER 7

Paul begins Romans 7 by leaning into the notion of a participatory life in Christ, one that states *because Jesus died, we have all died*. With regards to the Law, then, it becomes obsolete, says Paul:

> Are you unaware, brothers [...] that the Law dominates a man for whatever time he lives [...] Thus, my brothers, you too were made dead to the Law through the body of the Anointed so that you might come to be with another—the one who has been raised from the dead in order that we might bear fruit for God [because] now we have been released from the Law" (7:1–6, DBH).

Shockingly, Paul ends his initial argument by appealing to the "newness of Spirit," as opposed to "scripture's obsolescence." (7:6) This might come as a shock, especially for those who assume Paul is a champion of scripture and a defender of the inerrancy and infallibility of the text. However, Paul is also quite critical of not only a Judaizing application of the Law, but, as we explored in chapter 4, outright condemns it in many places—as do other New Testament authors.[8]

Notice how Paul teaches, both in Romans and elsewhere, that Christ has *fulfilled* rather than disregarded the Law, thus rendering it obsolete. As he says in 10:4: "Christ is the end of the Law." In Ephesians 2:15, Paul (or pseudo-Paul) also teaches that Christ, "broke down the barrier of the dividing wall [between Jew and Gentile] *by abolishing in his flesh* [...] *the Law of commandments contained in ordinances*, that in himself he might make the two into one new man, thus establishing peace" (emphasis ours).

Further, on not one, but two different occasions, the apostle explains the contrast between Law and grace in very radical terms. The first time he does this is in 2 Corinthians, where Paul creates the stark contrast as follows:

> Now if the ministry that brought death, which was engraved in letters on stone, [i.e., the law of Moses] came with glory, so that the Israelites could not look steadily at the face of Moses because of its glory, fading though it was, [the law is "fading"] will not the ministry of the Spirit [i.e., the new covenant of grace] be even more glorious? If the ministry that condemns men [the law] is glorious, how much more glorious is the ministry that brings righteousness [i.e., the gospel]? For what was glorious [the law] has no glory now in comparison with the surpassing glory. And if what was fading away [the law] came with glory, how much greater is the glory of that which lasts [the gospel of grace]![9]

To summarize, here is what Paul is telling us about the Law:

- It brings death.
- Its glory has been fading.
- It condemns.
- It *was* once glorious (past-tense).
- It currently has no glory (present-tense).
- It is fading away completely.

In contrast, Paul describes the gospel of grace like this:

- It is more glorious than the "old covenant."
- It brings righteousness.
- It has a glory that is surpassing.
- It is everlasting.

Another instance where Paul compares the "old" and "new" can be found in Galatians 4:

> The women (Hagar and Sarah) represent two covenants. One covenant is from Mount Sinai and bears children who are to be slaves: This is Hagar. Now Hagar stands for Mount Sinai in Arabia and corresponds to the present city of Jerusalem, because she is in slavery with her children. But the Jerusalem that is above is free, and she is our mother [...] But what does scripture say? "Get rid of the slave woman and her son, for the

> slave woman's son will never share in the inheritance with the free woman's son." Therefore, brothers and sisters, we are not children of the slave woman, but of the free woman.[10]

Again, to recap Paul's blunt words from Galatians, it is said that the Law:

- Comes from Mount Sinai (where the Ten Commandments were given).
- Bears children who are slaves.
- Corresponds to earthly Jerusalem.
- Is in slavery with her children.
- Should be cast out of our presence.
- Will not share in the inheritance of Christ.
- Is not our mother.

In contrast, of the "law" of grace, Paul writes how it:

- Bears children who are free.
- Is of the heavenly new Jerusalem.
- Is our true mother.
- Shares in the inheritance of Christ.

To drive the point even further, in other instances, Paul reiterates how:

"We are not under the Law" (6:14).[11]
"We are dead to the Law" (7:4).
"We are delivered from the Law" (7:6).

Therefore, says Paul, those who are in Christ are not under a strict adherence to the Ten Commandments but under a different law, writing: "Carry each other's burdens, and in this way you will fulfill the law of Christ."[12]

Okay, but what about the Jewish people? Are the people of Israel not chosen by God? Well, that depends on what you mean by "Israel" and "chosen." Paul points out to us that not everyone who claims to be Israel is truly Israel. As he would go on to write in 9:6: "It is not as though the word of God has failed. For not all those descended from Israel are Israelites." And again, as he argues in Galatians, the true children of Abraham are those who "in Christ," writing: "If you belong to Christ, then you are Abraham's seed, and heirs according to the promise."[13] In other words, what makes someone a child of Abraham is not about keeping the Law, or even being born Jewish. It is simply about being in Christ, which raises the question: "Who is in Christ?" That is what Paul wants to explain over the course of the next couple chapters of his letter.

Now, for those who are wondering about Jesus' statement regarding not coming to abolish the Law but to fulfill it—that not even a jot or tittle would pass from the Law until heaven and earth passed away—we are now going to take a closer look at this before we get back to our study of Romans 7–8.

The Meaning of Fulfillment

> *Do not think that I have come to abolish the Law or the Prophets; I have not come to abolish them but to fulfill them. I tell you the truth, until heaven and earth disappear, not the smallest letter, not the least stroke of a pen, will by any means disappear from the Law until everything is accomplished.*[14]

There are two qualifiers in the passage above: 1) the Law will not disappear until "heaven and earth disappear," and, 2) the Law will not disappear until "everything is accomplished." To that end, the natural question then becomes: Was everything accomplished? The simple answer to that is: *Yes!*

> *When he had received the drink, Jesus said, "It is finished." With that, he bowed his head and gave up his spirit.*[15]

So, on the cross, Jesus declares that he has accomplished his mission to "fulfill the Law," just as he set out to do, which is confirmed in his prayer to the Father before his death: "I have glorified you on earth by accomplishing the work you gave me to do."[16] What is the takeaway, then, according to the two qualifiers Jesus mentioned above? That since everything has been accomplished, the Law has now become obsolete.

LIFE IN CHRIST IN CHAPTER 8

As we focus our attention back to Romans, we will notice the conundrum that is the Law. On the one hand, sin brings death, so it is natural to desire the knowledge of iniquity. The Law does that, making it holy in some sense.

But, "when the commandment [Law] came, sin sprang to life and I died," says Paul (7:9).

This catch-22, whereby even those who love the Law of God will discover a different law in their body, one that wages war, taking us, "captive by the law of sin that is in (our) members." This causes Paul—and all of us—to cry out, "Who will deliver me from the body of this death?" The answer comes: "Grace to God through Jesus the Anointed, our Lord [...] for the law of the spirit of life in the Anointed One Jesus has freed you from the law of sin and death" (7:25; 8:2, DBH).

In the beginning of Romans 8, Paul expounds on the law of sin and death, and the fruit of walking according to the flesh as opposed to the spirit of Christ; but he is quick to remind us that "you are not of the flesh but rather of the spirit, since God's Spirit dwells in you" (8:9). His point being that, if you are alive, it is because, "the Spirit of the one who has raised Jesus from the dead dwells in you, [and that] he who raised the Anointed One Jesus from the dead will also make your mortal bodies live through the indwelling of his Spirit in you" (8:11, DBH).

At this point, we cannot ignore the verse between 9 and 11, where Paul adds, "but if one does not have the Spirit of the Anointed, this one is not his," simply because it is inconveniently placed between phrases that we like better. Paul is making a case and he is aware that his readers are not automatically predisposed to his thinking. So, he adds this verse, which suggests that there are some who are not in Christ. This, of course, is an idea that he wants to return to later, but for now, we are left with the possibility that there are some who are "in Christ" and some who are not. Although Paul will affirm in 8:16 that, "the Spirit itself testifies along with our spirit that we are God's children," the question of who is in Christ or not—or if it is even possible to exist apart from Christ—is something that Paul will answer shortly.

Divine Collaboration

Later in Romans 8, Paul famously affirms that, "all things work together for good for those who love God, who are called according to his purpose" (8:28). It may come as a surprise that this is not an accurate translation of the text. We may like to think that God is the one who makes everything work out in our favor as long we remain faithful, but that is not at all what is being said here. As famed New Testament scholar N.T. Wright explains, the verse should be translated a bit differently, explaining:

> It's a very dense bit of Greek and when we look at it, actually God is the subject of the sentence—that's the first thing—it's God who will work all things together but then the "working together"—the verb Paul uses here—means that God is taking those whom God loves as his partners [...] and the previous two verses explain who those partners are [...] because when he says "those who love God" he is referring to these who are lamenting, who are groaning in the groaning of all creation (8:26–27), who are resonating with the pain of the world, and Paul says that the Holy Spirit is indwelling them and the Spirit, too, is groaning with inarticulate yearning. That means that something is going on here; that within the world there is the Church [and] there is the Spirit groaning. Those who are holding on to that in lament, Paul says they are the ones who love God, and somehow God uses that lament, that prayer which is often a wordless prayer, a cry of pain; of not understanding, God uses *that* within his purposes for good; for larger good to come to the world. Which, in the passage, is about the renewal of all creation; the time when the whole creation will be set free [...] So it's a very dense verse, and it is

> full of hope, but it doesn't just mean we are passive and sitting back and saying, "well, this will all work out somehow," but we are very much praying often in agony or in lament and *we can be assured that God is working with us at those times* [...] *to bring good in the short and in the much longer term*"[17] (emphasis ours).

All this to say: It is not that God somehow makes everything work out in our favor in the end. Instead, God collaborates with us—as we intercede in the Spirit with groans that words cannot express—awakening us to our true identity as sons and daughters of God. When we undergo this transformation, we step into our identity as the incarnation of Christ in the world, working together with God to fulfill our mandate of bringing the kingdom of God to earth, here and now.[18]

And so, a better way to paraphrase this verse might be something closer to this:

> For we know that God, working together with those of us who have been touched by God's love, is yearning to bring good out of all the suffering and evil we see around us in our world today. This is our calling according to God's purpose: To collaborate with the Spirit of God within us, to bring his kingdom to earth, now.

That is why we should stop quoting this verse to suggest how God will somehow make everything work out in our favor. Instead, we should allow this verse to remind us that we are called to work together with God to bring joy, peace, healing, compassion, justice, and love to the world around us. We should begin to groan along with all creation for more justice, peace, and love. We should begin to groan along with the Spirit of God inside us for mercy, forgiveness, and grace.

Once our hearts and spirits are aligned with all of creation and with God's Spirit within, we will be resonating with the frequency that becomes the carrier wave of God's kingdom to earth. Working together with God we can transform the evils in this world into the good that God has always intended for us to experience. This will not happen if we do nothing. The world will not change until we change. Because, if we notice what Paul says in this same chapter a few verses earlier, the suffering in this world is not to be compared with the glory that is within each of us, and all creation is groaning for this to be released and revealed:

> For I consider that the sufferings of this present time are not worthy to be compared with the glory that is to be revealed to us. For the anxious longing of the creation waits eagerly for the revealing of the sons of God (8:18–19, DBH).

We usually read these verses as if they are about a heaven to come, but they are not. Paul does not place our future hope in the second coming of Christ, or the promise of heaven after we die. Not at all. He explicitly says that there is a glory waiting to be revealed *in us*.

It is not the return of Christ that all creation is yearning for. It is the moment when the sons and daughters of God are finally revealed and awakened into the fullness of our identity in Christ. We are the hands and feet of Jesus today. We are his body. Whatever we are doing is what Christ is doing. That is what it means to participate in Christ's resurrection, so let us stop waiting for Jesus to "come and fix it." Christ—and all creation—is groaning for us to wake up and start working all things together for good.

Those He Foreknew

Immediately following this section, we come across one of the more problematic teachings in the entire book of Romans: the doctrine of predestination. Or, perhaps we should say, the "apparent doctrine of predestination," since this is a prime example of how so many Christians over the past few hundred years have been reading Romans wrong. Let us take a closer look at the passage in question:

> For those whom he [God] foreknew he also predestined to be conformed to the image of his Son, in order that he might be the firstborn within a large family. And those whom he predestined he also called, and those whom he called he also justified, and those whom he justified he also glorified (8:29–30).

At first glance, these verses appear to suggest that God knew in advance who would be "conformed to the image of his Son," and that "those God predestined" are "God's elect" (8:33); but is that what Paul is really saying here? Has he indeed gone from suggesting that "all are saved" to "only some are saved?"

If we look at a different translation of the text, we find out that the above verses could easily be rendered the following way:

> Because those [God] knew in advance he then marked out in advance as being in conformity to the image of his Son, so that he might be firstborn among many brothers, and those he marked out in advance, these he then called; those he called, these proved upright; and those he proved upright, these he then glorified (8:29–30, DBH).

David Bentley Hart's translation again sheds some much-needed light on a difficult passage. In his translation, he notes that the phrase "being in conformity" is usually interpreted as "to be conformed to," which, even if it agrees with a certain brand of Reformed theology, is simply erroneous. As

Hart explains, "The phrase seems more naturally to mean that those whom God foreknew he then marked out as persons already conformed to the image of his Son. Much depends upon whether the prior 'delineation' or 'demarcation' of this conformity is understood as determining it or merely setting it apart."[19]

In other words, it makes a world of difference whether you translate the phrase as if God predestined some "to be conformed to the image of his Son," or as if God "marked out those in advance who were already being conformed to the image of his Son." The former translation suggests that God decides who would be conformed—and who would not—to the image of Christ, while the latter suggests that God merely recognized those who were already conformed to the image of Christ. We prefer the reading that allows for everyone to actively participate in choosing to be conformed to the image of Christ, rather than the view that a monergistic God does everything void of participation. Not only does the staunch predestination view contradict everything else that Paul argues for in Romans with regards to a participatory resurrection, it also creates a duality of "us and them," whereby some are in and some are out. As we move into Romans 9–11, we will argue that that is exactly the type of dualistic thinking Paul is in the process of refuting.

Questions and Answers

What follows next is a series of questions that Paul largely leaves unanswered:

> What then shall we say about these things? If God is for us, who is against us? He who did not even spare his own Son, but rather delivered him over on behalf of all of us, how shall he not grace us with all things along with him? Who will make an accusation against God's chosen ones? God is the one who vindicates. Who is the one who condemns? The Anointed One, Jesus? He who has died—or, rather, he who

> was raised? Who is at God's right hand? Who also intercedes for us? (8:31–34, DBH).

We maintain that these questions do not teach that Jesus is the one who condemns, but rather the very opposite. Notice that when Paul asks this question, "Who is the one who condemns?" that the answer is not, "The Anointed One, Jesus!" but, "The Anointed One, Jesus?" That is our clue that Paul thinks the idea that Jesus condemns us is outrageous and nonsensical. How can Jesus be the one who condemns us when Jesus is the one who died for us "while we were yet sinners?" How can Jesus be the one who condemns us when Jesus is the one who prayed, "Father, forgive all of them. They do not know what they are doing?"[20] How can Jesus be the one who condemns us when he is the one who was raised from the dead on our behalf and who appeared to his disciples saying, "Peace be with you!"[21] No, it cannot be Jesus who condemns us when it is Jesus who forgives us and pardons us and breathes peace over us and even now "intercedes for us" (8:34).

To drive his point home even further, in 8:35 Paul goes on to ask another important rhetorical question: "Who will separate us from the love of the Anointed? Shall afflictions or anguish, or persecution or famine or nakedness or peril or the sword?" To which he answers:

> For I have been persuaded that neither death nor life nor angels nor demons nor things present nor things to come nor powers, neither height nor depth nor any other creature will ever be able to separate us from the love of God that is in the Anointed, Jesus our Lord (8:38–39, DBH, paraphrased).

So, Paul ends Romans 8 by once more affirming that we are not condemned but loved by God, and that nothing can ever separate us from divine love. But what about that pesky False Teacher? We have not heard from him in a while, so it is about time for Paul to grapple one final time with his opponent, beginning in Romans 9.

Nine

Romans 9–11

God's Universal Mercy

Romans 9–11 marks the return of the False Teacher and therefore includes the final section of prosopopoeia in Romans. It is also where the apostle Paul brings everything together into his ultimate, triumphant conclusion regarding the question of who is "in" and who is "out" in the eyes of God. This portion of the text begins with an emotional plea to his "brothers and kindred according to the flesh [...] they who are Israelites," for whose sake he is willing to be cut off from Christ if such a thing were necessary for their salvation (9:3–4). Note that he does not say that such a thing is indeed necessary, only that his love for them is enough that he would be willing to lay down his own eternal soul for their sake. However, the hyperbolic analogy does leave us with the faintest suggestion as to whether the salvation of certain Jews is in doubt.

To begin, Paul enumerates the deep heritage of his people, beginning with their spiritual adoption as the children of God, to the covenants, the Law of Moses, the promises of God, the fathers of the faith, and, at last, the coming of the promised messiah—the Anointed One—before writing the following:

> Not, of course, that God's word has proved ineffectual. For not all of those who come from Israel are Israel (9:6).

What is he doing here? Put simply, Paul is answering the unspoken question he posed in 9:3 regarding the salvation of Israel and, more specifically, of those who reject Jesus as the Christ. If, as the scriptures promise, "all Israel shall be saved," then how can this be true if so many of those Israelites do not currently accept Jesus as their messiah? As we have already pointed out in greater detail above, Paul reminds us that not everyone who is ethnically or even religiously Jewish is necessarily an Israelite, adding, "...nor are all of them children because they are Abraham's seed," (9:7) which "means that it is not the children of the flesh who are the children of God, but the children of the promise are counted as descendants" (9:8).

UNCONDITIONAL ELECTION?

Next, Paul reminds his readers that God's mercy extends to those who have yet to be born, harkening back to the days when God chose Jacob to be blessed while still in his mother's womb. Here, we should stop and say something about Paul's use of the phrase, "Jacob I loved, but Esau I hated," (9:13) as it has been one of the most misused and misunderstood verses in this epistle. Most often, this potentially problematic phrase is used by hyper-Calvinists to suggest that God loves some people while hating others. This is a common mistake that has caused a lot of confusion.

First off, how can Paul say that God hates Esau when elsewhere in the New Testament we read that God *is* love, and as such, that it extends to everyone universally?[1] Reformed Calvinists would argue that 9:13 proves that God's love is *not* unconditional—that God does indeed hate some people while loving others based on nothing more than God's own capricious will. This is often linked to the passages we looked at in 8:29–30, which these same people argue teach that salvation is purely about election and predestination. So, if this is not the right way to understand these verses, then how can we read them the way Paul intends for us to?

We do this by first acknowledging how the question in 9:13 is really an echo of something written in Malachi 1:1–3, which is used as hyperbole to contrast the way the nation sprouting out from Jacob was blessed while the nation coming from Esau was not. It has nothing to do with the individual brothers, Jacob and Esau. In fact, if we go back and read the story of Jacob and Esau, we notice that they were *both* blessed by God with wives and children, land, and livestock, and that even though they fight to the point of having a falling out of biblical proportions, indeed end up reconciling with one another in the end. There is not one verse in the narrative to suggest that God "hated" Esau in any way—because if he did, how can he claim to love Jacob, given their eventual love for *each other*?[2] So, when Paul quotes this verse from Malachi, it is merely to point out that God has the right to decide who he will bless and to whom he will show mercy. That is the entire point of this phrase. And when he asks the rhetorical question in the very next verse, "What then shall we say? Is there injustice with God?" (9:14) he can respond by saying, "(As he tells Moses) 'I will have mercy on whomever I have mercy, and I will pity whomever I pity.'" Why? Because this is the point he is trying to make in the first place—not that God arbitrarily chooses to hate this person and love that one, but that God has mercy on whomever he shows mercy, and pities whomever he pities. When it comes to mercy and salvation, the emphasis is on God, not on the individual people in question.

Paul continues by adding another analogy of God's right to show mercy in the case of Pharaoh and, again, responds to that example by saying, "So then he has mercy on whomsoever he chooses, and he hardens the heart of whomsoever he chooses" (9:18).

This raises the question that Paul himself voices, "Why then does (God) still find fault? For who can resist his will?" The apostle responds with questions of his own:

> Who indeed are you, a human being, to argue with God? Will what is molded say to the one who molds it, "Why have you made me like this?" Has the potter no right over the clay, to make out of the same lump one object for special use and another for ordinary use? (9:20–21).

Or, to put it another way, "Who are you to question God's decision to show mercy to whomever he chooses?" What Paul is saying is that we do not get to argue about to whom God shows mercy and to whom God does not show mercy. This argument will be especially crucial to remember when Paul makes his final point at the end of Romans 11.

HYPOTHETICAL QUESTIONS

What Paul writes next is another pivotal statement that we want to stop and unpack before moving on to the rest of this chapter, as it is another crucial part of Romans that is quite often misunderstood. The verses in question read as follows:

> What if God, desiring to show his wrath and to make known his power, has endured with much patience the objects of wrath that are made for destruction; and what if he has done so in order to make known the riches of his glory for the objects of mercy, which he has prepared beforehand for glory? (9:22–23).

Once again, many Calvinists suggest that this text is telling us that God indeed does have a desire to "show his wrath and to make known his power" by fashioning "objects of wrath that are made for destruction." But is that what Paul is really suggesting? Hart sheds light on the case:

> The verse should be translated as if Paul were asking not whether God perhaps wished to display his indignation and therefore prepared vessels of wrath, but rather whether God, although inclined to show his indignation against sin, nevertheless tolerates vessels suitable for destruction, so that he will

> instead be able to display his mercy when the time comes for raising up vessels of mercy to fulfill his purposes.[3]

So, these verses are better translated like this:

> And what if God, though disposed to display his indignation and make known what is possible for him, tolerated with enormous magnanimity vessels of indignation, suitable for destruction, in order that he might also make known the wealth of his glory upon vessels of mercy that he had already prepared for glory, whom—us—he called not only from the Judaeans but from the Gentiles as well? (9:22–24, DBH).

Toward the end of Romans 9 (and prior to Paul's final diatribe with the False Teacher), the apostle, wanting to drive the point home that God's desire is to show mercy to everyone—both Jews and Gentiles—and to extend salvation to everyone—even those who reject him—uses scripture to point out that God's mercy is for the Gentiles and the unbelievers:

> As he also says to Hosea, "I will call the people not mine 'my people,' and her who is not beloved, 'Beloved'"; and "It shall be in the place where it was said [to them], 'You are not a people of mine': there they will be called sons of a living God." (9:25–26).

And for the people of Israel, God's mercy is expressed this way:

> And Isaiah cries out concerning Israel, "Though the number of the children of Israel were like the sand of the sea, only a remnant of them will be saved; for the Lord will execute his

> sentence on the earth quickly and decisively." And as Isaiah predicted, "If the Lord of hosts had not left survivors to us we would have fared like Sodom and been made like Gomorrah" (9:27–29).

At this point, the diatribe begins and the False Teacher reenters the scene. The debate continues at length (Paul's words are again in italics while those of the False Teacher are in bold):

> **What then shall we say? That Gentiles, not chasing after righteousness, seized hold of righteousness?** (9:30a, DBH).
>
> *Albeit, a righteousness coming from faithfulness* (9:30b, DBH).
>
> **While Israel, chasing after a Law of righteousness, failed to catch up to the Law?** (9:31, DBH).
>
> *Why? Because not out of faithfulness, but rather out of observances, they stumbled over the "stone of stumbling," just as has been written, "See, I set in Zion a stone of stumbling and a rock for faltering, and whoever has faith in him will not be put to shame"* (9:32–33, DBH).
>
> *Brothers, my heart's fond desire and prayer to God on their behalf is for salvation. For I testify of them that they have a zeal for God, but not according to knowledge; for, not knowing God's justice and seeking to set up their own, they did not become subject to God's justice. Because the end of the Law is the Anointed [Christ], for the purpose of uprightness for everyone having faith. For Moses writes of the Law's uprightness that: "The man*

who does these things will live by them." But the uprightness coming from faithfulness speaks thus: "Do not say in your heart, 'Who will ascend into heaven?'"—that is, to bring the Anointed down—or, "Who will descend into the abyss?"—that is, to bring the Anointed up from the dead. What does it say, rather? "The utterance is near you, in your mouth and in your heart"—that is, the utterance of the faith that we proclaim. Because, if you confess with your mouth "Jesus is Lord," and have faith in your heart that God raised him from the dead, you shall be saved. For one has faith in the heart for uprightness and confesses with the mouth for salvation. For the scripture says, "No one who has faith in him will be put to shame." For there is no distinction between Judaean and Greek. For the same one is Lord of all, with riches for all who call on him. For "Everyone who invokes the name of the Lord shall be saved" (10:1–13, DBH).

But how are they to call on one in whom they have not believed? And how are they to believe in one of whom they have never heard? And how are they to hear without someone to proclaim him? And how are they to proclaim him unless they are sent? (10:14–15a).

Just as has been written: "How lovely are the feet of those [announcing glad tidings of peace and] proclaiming glad tidings of good things" (10:15b, DBH).

But not all heeded the good tidings (10:16a, DBH).

Isaiah says, "Lord, who had faith in our report?" So, faith is from hearing, and hearing is by the utterance of the Anointed (10:16b–17, DBH).

But I say, "Did they not hear?" (10:18a, DBH).

Yes, indeed: "Their speech went out to all the earth, and their utterances to the ends of the inhabited world" (10:18b, DBH).

Again I ask, "Did Israel not understand?" (10:19a).

First Moses says, "I will make you jealous of those who are not a nation; with a foolish nation I will make you angry." Then Isaiah is so bold as to say, "I have been found by those who did not seek me; I have shown myself to those who did not ask for me." But of Israel he says, "All day long I have held out my hands to a disobedient and contrary people" (10:19b-21).

I ask, then, has God rejected his people? (11–1a).

Let it be not so! For I, too, am an Israelite, of Abraham's seed, of the tribe of Benjamin. God did not reject his people, whom he knew in advance. Or do you not know what scripture says regarding Elijah, how he made a plea with God against Israel? "Lord, they killed your prophets and razed your altars to the ground, and I was left behind alone and they seek my soul." Yet, what does the divine oracle tell him? "I reserved seven thousand men for myself, those who did not bend the knee to Baal." So, then, in the present time too a remnant has arisen according to the election of grace. And if by grace, then no longer from observances, since grace were then no longer grace. [And if from observances, it is no longer grace, since then observance were observance no longer.] What then? The mark Israel aims at, this it did not hit, but "election" did hit it; and the rest were hardened. As has been written, "God gave them a spirit of stupor, eyes that do not see, and ears that do not hear"—right up to the present

> *day. And David says, "Let their table come to serve as a snare and as a net and as a stumbling-block and as retribution for them, let their unseeing eyes be darkened, and their back forever bent down"* (11:1b–10, DBH).

> **So I ask, have they stumbled so as to fall?** (11:11).

> *Let it not be so! Rather, through their error comes salvation for the Gentiles, so as to provoke them to envy. But if their error is enrichment for the cosmos and their discomfiture enrichment for the Gentiles, how much more so the full totality of them?* (11:12–13, DBH).

PAUL'S CONCLUDING STATEMENTS

Turning away from his debate with the teacher of the Law, Paul then pivots to address the Gentile audience to whom this letter is primarily written, offering warnings to not think of themselves as better than the Israelites, since they are merely branches that have been grafted into the olive tree:

> Do not exult over the branches; rather, if you do exult, you do not support the root, but rather the root [supports] you [...] do not be haughtily minded, but fearful [respectful]. For if God did not spare the natural branches, neither will he spare you (11:18, 20b–21, DBH).

From here, Paul clears up a few of the questions posed in Romans 9—"Is there injustice on God's part?" (9:14) and "What if God, though disposed to display his indignation [against sin] and make known what is possible for him, tolerated with enormous magnanimity vessels of indignation, suitable for destruction, in order that he might also make known the wealth of his glory?" (9:22–23, DBH). He does this by speaking of the mysterious nature of God's mercy:

> *For I do not want you, brothers, to be ignorant of this mystery*, lest you be arrogant in yourselves: that a hardness has come upon one part of Israel until the full totality of the Gentiles enter in, *and thus all of Israel shall be saved* [...] For God's bestowals of grace and vocation are not subject to a change of heart" (11:25–26a, 29, DBH, emphasis ours).

As the chapter concludes, Paul is ready to offer a closing statement that will pull everything that he has argued up to this point together in one triumphant flourish:

> For, even as you once did not trust in God but have now received mercy through their [the Israelites] mistrust, so they now also have not trusted, to the end that, by the mercy shown you, they now might also receive mercy. *For God shut up everyone in obstinacy so that he might show mercy to everyone* (11:30–31, DBH, emphasis ours).

At last, Paul, makes it known that even those who are not predestined or elected will be saved by God's irresistible grace and mercy. As Hart explains:

> Paul affirms that the estrangement of the elect and "those who stumble" is a temporary providential arrangement that allows the "full totality" of Jews and Gentiles alike to enter in; and there, finally, he affirms that there is then no actual distinction

> of vessels of wrath from vessels of mercy: rather, all are bound in sin and all will receive mercy.[4]

This final crescendo at the end of Romans 11 concludes with a triumphant exultation of praise for God's incomprehensible goodness and inexpressible mercy to everyone, everywhere:

> O the depth of God's richness and wisdom and knowledge! How inscrutable his judgments and untraceable his paths! For "who has known the Lord's mind? Or how has become a counselor to him?" Who has given him anything in the past and will have it repaid him? Because from him and through him and to him is everything; to him the glory, unto the ages, amen (11:33–36, DBH).

If the Epistle to the Romans had ended here, Christians throughout the ages might have been less confused about the purpose of this letter or the heart of what Paul wanted to communicate in the first place. But such is not the case. Not to diminish the chapters that follow, our goal in saying this is to shine a distinctly bright spotlight on the gravitas of Romans 11—the crescendo to the story Paul has been laying out all throughout the first eleven chapters of his letter.

Beginning in Romans 1, when he provokes the righteous indignation of his readers only to expose their hypocrisy in 2:1–5, Paul dives straight into a debate with the False Teacher over the questions of whether it is necessary to keep the Law and whether God's promises to Israel have failed. From there, the apostle Paul makes the strongest case he possibly can that God's desire and intention is to save everyone, everywhere—Jew or Gentile, Christian or Pagan—regardless of what anyone has or has not done to deserve such unmerited grace. That though all have tasted "sin and death" stemming from Adam's selfish act, all will taste "life and righteousness" because of Christ's selfless one. To which, Paul boasts, "from him and through him and to him is everything; to him the glory, unto the ages, amen." (11:36, DBH)

Everything in Romans that follows this exuberant celebration of God's unbelievable goodness at the end of Romans 11 should be understood through the lens of this glorious mystery. It is to these chapters we now turn.

PART FOUR

Wrapping It All up with Romans 12–16

"The epistle to the Romans offers no new, strange, personal truth, but rather, the Truth which is old, familiar, and universal. It lays no claims to originality, nor does it pretend to be deeply spiritual. It cannot, however, be for this reason overlooked, for it possesses a real claim to serious consideration [...] It does not proclaim the authority of Paul; yet neither can it be dismissed when it is discovered that at best the whole is just—Paul. For, that Paul is not Christ, is a quite trivial, obvious truth; Christ, moreover, stands in no book, and to believe in the man who wrote the epistle or in what he wrote is out of the question: it is possible to believe only in God! This is precisely the thesis of the epistle."[1]

KARL BARTH

The Epistle to the Romans

Ten

Romans 12

In View of God's Mercy

Immediately after Paul's victory celebration at the end of Romans 11, where he extols the extravagant depths of God's love and grace in showing mercy to everyone and everywhere, he poses the question, "If everyone is saved, what's the point?" His answer is simple yet difficult to master:

> Therefore, I implore you brothers [and sisters] by God's mercies, to present your bodies as a living, holy, acceptable sacrifice to God, [which is] your rational [act of] worship; and do not be configured to this age, but be transformed by the renewal of the intellect, so you may test the will of God, which is good and acceptable and perfect (12:1–2, DBH).

So, because God's plan is to "imprison all in disobedience so that he may be merciful to all," Paul asks the church to respond by submitting their whole life to the glory of God, as this is an appropriate "rational [act of] worship" for those who are the recipients of such an excessively generous outpouring of God's boundless love. Our response should be to surrender ourselves to the will of God which is "good, acceptable and perfect," and our minds should be reconfigured to this new way of understanding who God is, *and*, subsequently, who we are. The ultimate act of *metanoia*[1] is when our minds are transformed and renewed by the reality of God's graciousness to us all.

Not only should we respond by submitting ourselves as living sacrifices to the God of love and mercy, we should also find ourselves driven to an unprecedented level of humility, as Paul says:

> For by the grace given to me I say to everyone among you not to think of yourself more highly than you ought to think, but to think with sober judgment, each according to the measure of faith that God has assigned (12:3).

Here, Paul turns to matters of how God's mercy should inspire *koinonia*[2] among us all. This realization that we are all the children of God, regardless of whether we are Jew or Gentile, slave or free, male or female, gives us hope and joy that through Christ we are all equally loved, adored, treasured, accepted, and welcomed in the Father's eyes. Therefore, we should recognize "we, who are many, are one body in Christ, and individually we are members one of another" (12:5).

This idea that we are "members of one another" is fascinating because it communicates the reality that to be a member of the body of Christ is to be a member of one another. The body of Christ is *us*, and we all belong to the other. Christ has no body but yours and you have no body but Christ's. They/we are one and the same, so whatever we are doing is what Christ is doing in the world. We all have a shared humanity and a shared divinity that cannot be separated.

From here, Paul shares an alternate version of something that is also emphasized in 1 Corinthians 12:28 and Ephesians 4:11–13. In the following lists, please note the differences and similarities between them:

- Romans 12:6–7 (7 gifts): "We have gifts that differ according to the grace given to us: *prophecy*, in proportion to faith; *ministry*, in ministering; *the teacher*, in teaching; *the exhorter*, in exhortation; *the giver*, in generosity; *the leader*, in diligence; *the compassionate*, in cheerfulness."

- 1 Corinthians 12:28 (8 gifts): "And God has placed in the church first of all *apostles*, second *prophets*, third *teachers*, then *miracles*, then *gifts of healing*, *of helping*, *of guidance*, and of *different kinds of tongues*."

- Ephesians 4:11–13: (5 gifts): "So Christ himself gave the *apostles*, the *prophets*, the *evangelists*, the *pastors* and *teachers*, to equip his people for works of service, so that the body of Christ may be built up until we all reach unity in the faith and in the knowledge of the Son of God and become mature, attaining to the whole measure of the fullness of Christ."

Many modern Protestants and other Bible teachers mistakenly focus on the passage from Ephesians (ignoring the lists in Romans and 1 Corinthians) to promote something they call the Five-Fold Ministry. Perhaps it is because the list featured in Ephesians is the only one that includes the mention of a pastor, or perhaps because they dislike the mention of "compassion" or "helping" or "tongues" in those other lists. Whatever the case, the point we need to understand is that Paul sent slightly different lists to different groups of Christians in different countries. What this tells us is that Paul did not have one single formula for what gifts were more important than others. He does not even seem to remember what, exactly, he has said to the other churches in his previous letters. Instead, he shares what, in the moment, seems important to share with that group of people in that place and time.

Nevertheless, another common mistake is to see these lists as hierarchical, as if the apostles have authority over the prophets, who have authority over the evangelists, and so on. When Paul says in 1 Corinthians, "God has placed in the church first of all apostles, second prophets, third teachers..." he is speaking in chronological terms rather than hierarchical ones. In other words, the apostles of Christ came first because they were the ones sent out to establish churches. After that, those with the gift of prophecy began to proclaim the gospel of Christ, and then, after that, teachers began to help people understand the finer points of the good news, and so on. The early Christians understood that Jesus strongly condemned the practice of "lording over" one another to his disciples as he stressed, not once but twice, that it should "not be so among you":

> Jesus called them and said to them, "You know that among the Gentiles those whom they recognize as their rulers lord it over them, and their great ones are tyrants over them. But it is not so among you; but whoever wishes to become great among you must be your servant, and whoever wishes to be first among you must be slave of all. For the Son of Man came not to be served but to serve, and to give his life a ransom for many."[3]

And again:

> But he said to them, "The kings of the Gentiles lord it over them; and those in authority over them are called benefactors. But not so with you; rather the greatest among you must become like the youngest, and the leader like one who serves. For who is greater, the one who is at the table or the one who serves? Is it not the one at the table? But I am among you as one who serves."[4]

So, the apostles understood that, within the body of Christ, they were not to wield authority over one another but were to serve the other in love and humility (just as Jesus did). It was only later that this concept of mutual submission to one another in the body of Christ became abandoned in favor of the rule of the bishop, and even further along, the priest and the pastor.

The verses that follow Paul's list of gifts within the body of Christ are all focused on the necessity of love for one another. These exhortations are drenched in the teachings of Jesus and dripping with the ideas found in the Sermon on the Mount:

> Let love be genuine; hate what is evil, hold fast to what is good; love one another with mutual affection; outdo one another in showing honor. Do not lag in zeal, be ardent in spirit, and serve the Lord. Rejoice in hope, be patient in suffering, persevere in prayer. Contribute to the needs of the saints; extend hospitality to strangers. Bless those who persecute you; bless and do not curse them. Rejoice with those who rejoice, weep with those who weep. Live in harmony with one another; do not be haughty, but associate with the lowly; do not claim to be wiser than you are. Do not repay anyone evil for evil but take thought for what is noble in the sight of all. If it is possible, so far as it depends on you, live peaceably with all. Beloved, never avenge yourselves, but leave room for the wrath of God; for it is written, "Vengeance is mine, I will repay, says the Lord." No, "if your enemies are hungry, feed them; if they are thirsty, give them something to drink; for by doing this you will heap burning coals on their heads." Do not be overcome by evil but overcome evil with good (12:9-21).

Note that when Paul challenges the Christians in Rome to "love one another with mutual affection [and to] outdo one another in showing honor," it almost sounds like he wants them to make a game or a competition out of who can be the most loving and honoring among them. Given there is nothing to boast in but Christ, he is *not* challenging them to be prideful—"I'm more loving than you are"—but in the sense of sincerely and honestly expressing genuine love for one another in practical ways.

Finally, the oft-quoted verse about feeding your enemies and giving them water to drink to "heap burning coals upon their heads" needs to be addressed before we wrap up this chapter. Assuredly, Paul is not saying, "Here's how to really make someone you hate feel the pain." Rather, he is simply stating, "We have a new way of getting even: by loving people until they are transformed by Christ." In other words, the best way to destroy your enemy is to make them your friend.

IN CLOSING

This chapter began with a rhetorical question posed by the church: "If everyone is saved, what is the point?" Throughout Romans 12, Paul answers the question by declaring that the church in Rome must submit to one another out of their love for Christ and each other, but what comes next in Romans 13 is a reminder of how they are to submit to the higher authorities—namely the Roman Empire. In short, Romans 12 is all about the Church. Romans 13 is all about the State. Let us look at the differences now.

Eleven

Romans 13

Submission to Authorities

> Let every person be subject to the governing authorities; for there is no authority except from God, and those authorities that exist have been instituted by God (13:1).

American Protestants love to quote Romans 13—especially the verse above, doubly so when Republicans are in office—as proof that obedience to the State is required, that passing laws to enforce Christian doctrines is acceptable, and that joining the military is part of following Christ. That is not at all what Paul wants to communicate here, but we need to break it down to understand why.

First, when Paul says that "every person [should] be subject to the governing authorities," he is merely suggesting that Christians in Rome should not engage in violent rebellion against the empire. Zealots had a strong voice in the occupied territories under Roman authority and Paul's concern was that some of those who were part of the church in Rome might be tempted to violently resist those authorities. This does not mean that Christians should fail in resisting the Roman Empire at all. It simply means that their resistance—like the resistance that Jesus mimetically modeled—should be creatively nonviolent and quietly subversive. Violent opposition brings a violent response. Jesus most certainly did not submit to the Roman authorities. In fact, he was crucified as a revolutionary who defied Rome's authority—but his defiance was not violent. It was creative. It was subversive. It was unconventional. But it was not violent.

Paul wants to make sure that the Roman assembly is not viewed by the governing authorities as an insurrectionist group of rebels that need to be put down. This is about the preservation of the church in Rome. So, when he says the following, it is a reminder to keep their noses clean and remain obedient to the law so they do not end up in prison ... or worse: "Whoever resists authority resists what God has appointed, and those who resist will incur judgment. For rulers are not a terror to good conduct, but to bad" (13:2–3).

Keep in mind that, at the time Paul wrote this letter to the church in Rome, the emperor on the throne was Nero. Nero was the most cruel, sadistic, and brutal ruler that Rome had ever known. He murdered his mother and two wives. He persecuted the early Christians. He even set fire to Rome to make room to expand his palace and martyred both the apostle Peter and even Paul himself. Everyone was quite aware of the need to tread softly around someone like Nero. To that end, when Paul says that the government is "God's servant for your good" (13:4a), he is doing two things: First, he is establishing what a truly just ruler should look like, and, second, he is quietly pointing out just how far the current ruler (Nero) falls short of that godly standard.

> But if you do what is wrong, you should be afraid, for the authority does not bear the sword in vain! It is the servant of God to execute wrath on the wrongdoer (13:4b).

To be clear, whenever a ruler punishes those who do good, that ruler is not bearing the sword appropriately; he is "bearing the sword in vain!" Now, notice what Paul says next about executing "wrath on the wrongdoer." This raises the questions: "What if the 'wrongdoer' is the emperor? Who will 'execute wrath' on him?" Paul's answer to this question should still linger in the air from last few verses that ended Romans 12 above:

> Beloved, never avenge yourselves, but leave room for the wrath[1] [of God]; for it is written, "Vengeance is mine, I will repay, says the Lord." No, "if your enemies are hungry, feed them; if they are thirsty, give them something to drink; for by doing this you will heap burning coals on their heads." Do not be overcome by evil, but overcome evil with good (12:19–21).

In other words, do not take vengeance upon the Roman government yourself, says Paul. Leave room for God to bring "wrath on the evildoer" (13:4b) because God has said, "I will repay" (13:19).[2] Our task is simply this: To love our enemies and to overcome evil with good.

Here, in Romans 13, Paul wants to explain why this nonviolent resistance to evil is especially necessary when it comes to how they respond to the excessive evils of Nero's Empire.

Submission to Roman authority—even Nero's authority—is a necessity "on account of outrage [and] on account of conscience as well." Why? Because our submission to that authority as if they were "God's servant for [our] good" (13:4b) only emphasizes the fact that they are failing in that regard, and this failure (which our obedience quietly points to) is calling attention to the need for God to raise up another "servant of God to execute wrath on the wrongdoer," (13:5) which, in this case, is Nero himself. And when that judgment against Nero comes—and it eventually does come—those who remained obedient to that unjust Roman authority can stand pure with a clear conscience.

(In case you are curious, when Roman senator Vindex rebelled against Nero, with support from the eventual Roman emperor Galba, Nero was declared a public enemy and condemned to death for his crimes. In response, Nero fled Rome and committed suicide soon after. So, God's judgments against him came to pass as Paul promised they would, and the church in

Rome continued to thrive and grow until it eventually became the seat of power for the Church—for better or *worse*—under Constantine.)

Paul's admonition in Romans 13 is for the Church in Rome to resist violence and to pay their taxes like good citizens:

> For the same reasons [wrath and conscience] you [should] also pay taxes, for the authorities are God's servants, busy with this very thing [administering justice]. Pay to all what is due to them—taxes to whom taxes are due, revenue to whom revenue is due, respect to whom respect is due, honor to whom honor is due. Owe no one anything, except to love one another; for the one who loves another has fulfilled the law (13:6–8, DBH).

Again, Paul is subtly pointing out the need to remain obedient to the government by paying taxes while also quietly acknowledging that they should pay "respect to whom respect is due and honor to whom honor is due." In other words, pay Nero the taxes you owe him, but you do not owe him your respect or your honor. He is not worthy of those things. However, the one thing we do owe Nero, and everyone else, is simply this: love!

> The commandments, "You shall not commit adultery; You shall not murder; You shall not steal; You shall not covet;" and any other commandment, are summed up in this word, "Love your neighbor as yourself." Love does no wrong to a neighbor; therefore, love is the fulfilling of the law (13:9–10).

Just as Jesus did in Luke 10:27 and Matthew 22:37, the apostle Paul summarizes the Law as *loving one another as we love ourselves.* This love for one another is how we show that we are the children of God because God is love.

Nevertheless, contrary to what you may have heard, the early church did not always agree on everything. In fact, they disagreed on many points of doctrine for the first few hundred years and beyond. But the one thing the early Christians unanimously agreed on was this: Jesus commanded us to love our enemies and not to use violence.

We find this teaching most plainly in the Sermon on the Mount:

> You have heard that it was said, "An eye for an eye and a tooth for a tooth." *But I say to you, Do not resist an evildoer. But if anyone strikes you on the right cheek, turn the other also ... You have heard that it was said, "You shall love your neighbor and hate your enemy." But I say to you, Love your enemies and pray for those who persecute you, so that you may be children of your Father in heaven*; for he makes his sun rise on the evil and on the good, and sends rain on the righteous and on the unrighteous. For if you love those who love you, what reward do you have? (Matthew 5:38–39, 43-46, emphasis ours).

Early Christians took these teachings to heart and endured persecution without retaliation. They suffered under both political and religious persecution without responding violently. In fact, we have no reports of any Christians responding to their enemies with violence, but instead have dozens of statements from early church fathers over several hundred years affirming the radical teaching of enemy love and creative nonviolence. For example, here are a few quotes from first and second-century Christian writers about the posture of nonviolence in the early Church:

Tertullian: The Lord, in disarming Peter, disarmed every soldier.

Origen: Christians could never slay their enemies. For the more that kings, rulers, and peoples have persecuted them everywhere, the more Christians have increased in number and grown in strength.

Lactantius: Wherever arms have glittered, they must be banished and exterminated from thence.

Clement of Alexandria: As simple and quiet sisters, peace and love require no arms. For it is not in war, but in peace, that we are trained.

Tatian: I do not wish to be a king; I am not anxious to be rich; I decline military command... Die to the world, repudiating the madness that is in it.

Justin Martyr: We who formerly used to murder one another now refrain from even making war upon our enemies.

Aristides: Whatever Christians would not wish others to do to them, they do not to others. And they comfort their oppressors and make them their friends; they do good to their enemies. Through love towards their oppressors, they persuade them to become Christians.

Hippolytus of Rome: A soldier of the civil authority must be taught not to kill men and to refuse to do so if he is command-

> ed and to refuse to take an oath. If he is unwilling to comply, he must be rejected for baptism. A military commander or civic magistrate must resign or be rejected. If a believer seeks to become a soldier, he must be rejected, for he has despised God.
>
> **Ignatius of Antioch:** There is nothing better than peace, in which all warfare of things in heaven and things on earth is abolished.
>
> **Irenaeus:** The new covenant that brings back peace and the law that gives life have gone forth over the whole earth, as the prophets said..." These people formed their swords and war lances into plowshares," that is, into instruments used for peaceful purposes. So now, they are unaccustomed to fighting, so when they are struck, they offer also the other cheek.
>
> **Arnobius:** We would rather shed our own blood than stain our hands and our conscience with that of another.
>
> **Athenagoras of Athens:** We have rejected such spectacles as the Coliseum. How then, when we do not even look on killing lest we should contract guilt and pollution, can we put people to death?

This short list of quotations spanning the first 300 years of church history should be enough to give you an idea about how the early Christians understood the nonviolent way of Christ. They believed that loving our enemies meant that we should not kill them.

And so, considering all of this, it is entirely misguided to attempt to use anything Paul says in Romans 13 as an endorsement of any semblance of violence among Christians. It simply was not taught or practiced by anyone who followed Jesus until the time of Emperor Constantine when the church underwent a radical reformation away from the practice of Christianity to an emphasis on the doctrines of Christianity.[3]

Paul's point in Romans 13 is that when the State wields the power of the sword for our good it is doing a service. When it misuses that power, our response is not to respond with more violence but to continue in the path of Christ which is about overcoming darkness with light and evil with love. He also wants us to see that it is the State—not the Church—that carries the sword. The Church carries the cross of Christ which only kills the ones who carry it.

Now, let us turn our attention to Romans 14.

Twelve

Romans 14

Let Everyone Be Convinced in Their Own Minds

Paul kicks off the next chapter with a line that most of us skip right over: "Welcome those who are weak in faith, but not for the purpose of quarreling over opinions" (14:1).

His concern for the Roman Church is that they "outdo one another in showing honor" (12:10) and here he wants to expound upon this notion with greater detail. Namely, when it comes to matters of doctrine and faith practices, he does not want them to waste any time arguing and debating with one another over what foods they can eat or what things they can drink, or what religious holidays they observe. In case you were not aware, these were very practical concerns at the time—as we see in 1 Corinthians, when Paul must respond to a conflict about whether it was a sin to eat meat that was sacrificed to a pagan idol:

> So then, about eating food sacrificed to idols: We know that "An idol is nothing at all in the world" and that "There is no God but one." But not everyone possesses this knowledge. Some people are still so accustomed to idols that when they eat sacrificial food they think of it as having been sacrificed to a god, and since their conscience is weak, it is defiled. But food does not bring us near to God; we are no worse if we do not eat, and no better if we do. Be careful, however, that the exercise of your rights does not become a stumbling block to the weak.[1]

This internal conflict in the Corinthian church about eating meat appears to have been a controversy in the Roman church as well. In both places, Paul argues that the highest priority is not to determine who is right and who is wrong. Instead, he argues that what matters most is to keep unity in the family of God by showing mutual love and respect for one another, regardless of what you believe to be true or false. In other words, Paul suggests that unity in the body of Christ is not about agreement but love.

Paul tells the Church in Rome what he told the Church in Corinth:

> Some believe in eating anything, while the weak eat only vegetables. Those who eat must not despise those who abstain, and those who abstain must not pass judgment on those who eat; for God has welcomed them [...] If your brother or sister is being injured by what you eat, you are no longer walking in love. Do not let what you eat cause the ruin of one for whom Christ died (14:12–3, 15).

Maintaining the unity of love in the body of Christ is of much greater importance than shaming those who eat differently, or crowning those who eat another way with honor. As Paul says in Romans 14:5, when it comes to arguments and disagreements over these petty things: "Let all be fully convinced in their own minds." In other words, if you think you are right, you are right. But leave everyone else alone to make up their own minds. As he says in 14:1: The point is to extend hospitality to everyone, "but not for the purpose of quarreling over opinions."

Too many Christians today ignore Paul's advice here. They are all about drafting up their statements of faith and enforcing those doctrines on everyone who wants to become a member of their church. They are not interested in allowing everyone to "be fully convinced in their own minds." Instead, they want to make sure that no one dares to think for themselves or have their own opinions about what is sinful and what is not. They believe that unity is based on agreement and they are willing to enforce that agreement on threat of expulsion from the community. Even though, in Paul's mind, unity is a choice based on mutual love and respect for everyone. He believes that the church can enjoy unity without first agreeing on whether it is a sin to eat meat sacrificed to idols, or whether it is necessary to observe Jewish feasts and festivals like Passover or Rosh Hashanah. This is why he says, "Some judge one day to be better than another, while others judge all days to be alike ... Those who observe the day, observe it in honor of the Lord [...] The belief that you hold on to for yourself, hold it before God" (14:5–6, 22 DBH).

Some of those in the Roman Church assuredly came from a Jewish background. These people felt it was important to continue observing Jewish holidays. Others did not. Paul's point is that they are all free to observe—or not to observe—those holidays. If they do, they do it "in honor of the Lord" and if they do not, it is not a sin.

Either way, those who practice and those who do not practice are both one in Christ and that unity matters more than who is right and who is wrong.

Amid this teaching, Paul again reminds the Christians in Rome of what he had said earlier at the end of Romans 11 about how God's plan is to save everyone, everywhere, when he says:

> For it has been written, "As I live," says the Lord, "every knee shall bow to me, and every tongue shall joyfully praise [*exomologeo*] God." So then, each of us will be accountable to God (14:11–12).

That term, *exomologeo*,[2] suggests that everyone, everywhere will bow their knee to God and joyfully—not through gritted teeth or under compulsion, but willingly and gladly—confess the goodness of God at the judgment.

So, considering this, let us not get distracted by petty arguments over food or feasts or festivals. These things do not matter. What matters is that God loves all of us and has saved all of us and that we are one with God and with one another.

> Let us therefore no longer pass judgment on one another, but resolve instead never to put a stumbling block or hindrance in the way of another. I know and am persuaded in the Lord Jesus that nothing is unclean in itself; but it is unclean for anyone who thinks it unclean ... For the kingdom of God is not food and drink but righteousness and peace and joy in the Holy Spirit ... Let us then pursue what makes for peace and for mutual edification (14:13–14, 17, 19).

Paul is nearly finished with what wants to say to the Church in Rome. Let us see what that might be.

Thirteen

ROMANS 15

Paul's Closing Thoughts

PAUL BEGINS TO WRAP up his letter to the Romans by focusing on a few final points: 1) a reminder to prioritize unity in the body of Christ, one based on love rather than agreement (15:1–7); 2) a reminder of God's promise to redeem everyone—both Jews and Gentiles alike (15:8–13); 3) a defense of his own ministry to the Gentiles (15:14–24); and finally, 4) an appeal for generosity in giving financially to support the mother church in Jerusalem (15:25–29).

As we begin to land the plane, let us look at these one at a time.

UNITY BASED ON LOVE

Pointing to Jesus as our example, Paul urges the Roman congregations to love their neighbor as Christ loved us:

> We who are strong ought to put up with the failings of the weak, and not to please ourselves. Each of us must please our neighbor for the good purpose of building up the neighbor. For Christ did not please himself; but, as it is written, "The insults of those who insult you have fallen on me ... May the God of steadfastness and encouragement grant you to live in harmony with one another, in accordance with Christ Jesus, so that together you may with one voice glorify the God and Father of our Lord Jesus Christ. Welcome one another, there-

> fore, just as Christ has welcomed you, for the glory of God" (15:1–3; 5–7).

This is quite similar to what Paul says to the church in Philippi:

> If then there is any encouragement in Christ, any consolation from love, any sharing in the Spirit, any compassion and sympathy, make my joy complete: be of the same mind, having the same love, being in full accord and of one mind. Do nothing from selfish ambition or conceit, but in humility regard others as better than yourselves. Let each of you look not to your own interests, but to the interests of others. Let the same mind be in you that was in Christ Jesus, who, though he was in the form of God, did not regard equality with God as something to be exploited, but emptied himself, taking the form of a slave, being born in human likeness. And being found in human form, he humbled himself and became obedient to the point of death—even death on a cross.[1]

Overall, Paul wants the Church in Rome (as in Philippi and other regions) to be known for their extravagant love for one another, and for the people in their community. He wants this love to be genuine, not forced or rehearsed, but sincerely flowing from their hearts as they consider the beautiful truth of God's extravagant love for all humanity.

GOD'S PROMISE TO REDEEM EVERYONE

After pointing them to the love that Christ has for them as a reason for loving one another, Paul reminds the Church in Rome of God's promise to redeem everyone, everywhere with some creative references to various Hebrew scriptures regarding the Gentiles:

> For I tell you that Christ has become a servant of the Jews on behalf of God's truth, so that the promises made to the patriarchs might be confirmed and, moreover, that the Gentiles might glorify God for his mercy. As it is written: "Therefore I will praise you among the Gentiles; I will sing the praises of your name." Again, it says, "Rejoice, you Gentiles, with his people." And again, "Praise the Lord, all you Gentiles; let all the peoples extol him." And again, Isaiah says, "The Root of Jesse will spring up, one who will arise to rule over the nations; in him the Gentiles will hope." May the God of hope fill you with all joy and peace as you trust in him, so that you may overflow with hope by the power of the Holy Spirit (15:8–13).

As we explored in chapter 4, all the above references following the phrases, "As it is written..." are creatively *misquoted* by Paul to emphasize the mercy of God to the Gentiles while intentionally editing out all references to the wrath and vengeance of God *against* the Gentiles. This is no accident. Paul was a "Pharisee of Pharisees"[2] who knew the Law and the Hebrew scriptures by heart. His selective quotations of the passages in 2 Samuel 22:50, Psalm 18:49, Deuteronomy 32:43, Isaiah 66:10, Psalm 117:1, and Isaiah 11:10 are quite intentional. He removes all references to the destruction and humiliation of Gentile and pagan nations in those passages and quotes only the verses that reference the rejoicing of the Gentiles and their collective praise of God's name for his infinite mercies. This audacious retelling of the story to prioritize God's goodness over all references to God's wrath in those passages is justified by what Paul has concluded in the previous chapters: that God's plan is to save everyone, everywhere.

APOSTLE TO THE GENTILES

After creatively reframing the Hebrew scriptures to speak of God's boundless love for the Gentiles, Paul affirms his priestly calling to preach the good news of the Kingdom to them:

> Yet I have written you quite boldly on some points to remind you of them again, because of the grace God gave me to be a minister of Christ Jesus to the Gentiles. He gave me the priestly duty of proclaiming the gospel of God, so that the Gentiles might become an offering acceptable to God, sanctified by the Holy Spirit. Therefore I glory in Christ Jesus in my service to God (15:15–17).

In fact, as Paul explains, it is his response to this heavenly calling that has prevented him from visiting them in person:

> I will not venture to speak of anything except what Christ has accomplished through me in leading the Gentiles to obey God by what I have said and done—by the power of signs and wonders, through the power of the Spirit of God. So from Jerusalem all the way around to Illyricum, I have fully proclaimed the gospel of Christ. It has always been my ambition to preach the gospel where Christ was not known, so that I would not be building on someone else's foundation ... This is why I have often been hindered from coming to you (15:18–20; 22).

However, Paul finally feels as if his work may have come to an end so that he can, at last, travel to Rome in person to meet them face to face:

> But now that there is no more place for me to work in these regions, and since I have been longing for many years to visit you, I plan to do so when I go to Spain. I hope to see you while passing through and to have you assist me on my journey there, after I have enjoyed your company for a while. Now, however, I am on my way to Jerusalem in the service of the Lord's people there (15:23–25).

A GIFT TO JERUSALEM'S CHURCH

Here, Paul makes mention of his next missionary journey to carry an offering to the church in Jerusalem:

> At present, however, I am going to Jerusalem in a ministry to the saints; for Macedonia and Achaia have been pleased to share their resources with the poor among the saints at Jerusalem. They were pleased to do this, and indeed they owe it to them; for if the Gentiles have come to share in their spiritual blessings, they ought also to be of service to them in material things. So, when I have completed this, and have delivered to them what has been collected, I will set out by way of you to Spain; and I know that when I come to you, I will come in the fullness of the blessing of Christ (15:25–29).

What is fascinating about his trip to Jerusalem is the fact that the exuberant outpouring of love among the believers there—as recorded in Acts 2—has now led them deeper into poverty together. As more and more people sold their property and laid it at the apostles' feet to provide food, shelter, and clothing for the poor among them, their resources have now run out and they must depend on an outpouring of that same exuberant generosity from their brothers and sisters across the Roman Empire to survive. Some may suggest that this proves that the Acts 2 model of voluntaryist communism is a failure, but we would rather see it as a natural effect of how love for one another is intended to spread until everyone, everywhere, truly cares for those in need based on an awareness of our unity in Christ and our shared humanity. So, from the beginning, it was always the plan for the spontaneous sharing of "all things in common" to spread outward so that everyone would eventually "sell all their possessions and goods and distribute them to all as any had need."[3] This was not a failure of Christian charity but a declaration of victory—that this outpouring of love should spread to cover the whole earth as the gospel itself had.

Paul ends Romans 15 with a somber note:

> I appeal to you, brothers and sisters, by our Lord Jesus Christ and by the love of the Spirit, to join me in earnest prayer to God on my behalf, that I may be rescued from the unbelievers in Judea, and that my ministry to Jerusalem may be acceptable to the saints, so that by God's will I may come to you with joy and be refreshed in your company (15:30–32).

Sadly, Paul's prayer is never answered. The "unbelievers in Judea" will end up seizing and arresting him and he would spend rest of his life in a Roman prison, never making that trip to Spain. Somewhere between 62 and 64 CE, Paul would die in that very same prison.

Fourteen

Romans 16

Greetings and Farewell

Paul ends his letter by taking the time to honor his fellow workers in the faith, beginning with Phoebe, the woman who would deliver the letter to the Romans in person and who would most likely go on to read the entire thing out loud to everyone as they listened intently.

In 16:2, Paul refers to her as a *diákonos* (or deacon) and as a *prostatis,* which is the Greek word for "ruler" or "leader." Such language is significant because it means she held a position of great authority and influence within the church. From here, Paul mentions several other names of fellow Christians—both men *and* women—who have been doing exemplary work as faithful servants:

> Greet Priscilla and Aquila, who work with me in Christ Jesus, and who risked their necks for my life, to whom not only I give thanks, but also all the churches of the Gentiles. Greet also the church in their house. Greet my beloved Epaenetus, who was the first convert in Asia for Christ. Greet Mary, who has worked very hard among you. Greet Andronicus and Junia, my relatives who were in prison with me; they are prominent among the apostles, and they were in Christ before I was. Greet Ampliatus, my beloved in the Lord. Greet Urbanus, our co-worker in Christ, and my beloved Stachys. Greet Apelles, who is approved in Christ. Greet those who belong to the family of Aristobulus. Greet my relative Herodion. Greet those

> in the Lord who belong to the family of Narcissus. Greet those workers in the Lord, Tryphaena and Tryphosa. Greet the beloved Persis, who has worked hard in the Lord. Greet Rufus, chosen in the Lord; and greet his mother—a mother to me also. Greet Asyncritus, Phlegon, Hermes, Patrobas, Hermas, and the brothers and sisters who are with them. Greet Philologus, Julia, Nereus and his sister, and Olympas, and all the saints who are with them. Greet one another with a holy kiss. All the churches of Christ greet you (16:1–16).

We must make note of the fact that the mention of Junia (16:7) has been, and continues to be, the cause of much consternation for Christian misogynists who, sadly, are so vexed by the idea that Paul could dare to mention an apostle as a normative position for *women* that they went so far as to change Junia into a man for several centuries until later translators finally admitted that Junia was indeed a woman—and yes, *"of note among the apostles."*

Incidentally, the first person to argue that Junia was male was *Giles* of Rome (1243–1316, of no relation to Keith Giles). But, according to Hart, this assertion "can be safely dismissed as nonsense ... [because] Junia the Apostle was a woman,"[1] going on to add that there is "no instance anywhere in the vast literary remains of antiquity, or of any period within the Greek or Latin tongues, of Junias as a masculine name."[2]

As often as Paul is lumped in with those early Christians who wanted to silence women, however, the fact remains: *he was quite vocal about the importance of women in the formation of the Christian faith.* In fact, without Paul's mention of so many of them by name, we would not know they existed or that they served as deacons, elders, prophets, teachers, and apostles.[3] Other examples of where Paul honors women in his writings are as follows:

1. **Tabitha:** An early disciple of Jesus who made clothing for the poor and served others in love.[4]

2. **Priscilla:** A "co-worker in the service of Christ" with Paul who, along with her husband Aquila, taught the apostle Apollos about the Holy Spirit, also travelling with Paul on his missional journeys.[5]

3. **Lydia:** A Gentile convert to Judaism who heard Paul speak and followed Jesus. She was an entrepreneur, even pastoring a church in her home.[6]

4. **Euodia and Scyntyche:** Two women who "labored side by side with Paul in the gospel together with Clement and the rest of Paul's fellow workers..."[7]

Now, as to one of the main passages that appear to mark Paul as one who forbade women to speak in the church, let us take a closer look:

> I do not permit a woman to teach in order to have authority over a man; she must be silent.[8]

First, as we mentioned in chapter 1, this passage is likely *not* written by Paul. Nevertheless, in the Greek language, the phrase is worded like this: "I am not now at this time allowing a woman to teach," which suggests that at other times the writer *did* allow women to teach. We know full well that elsewhere Paul proudly affirms the teaching and prophetic ministry of women, so something other than out-and-out misogyny must be going on here.

For context, 1 Timothy begins by telling us that there are certain individuals in this church who are causing division and trouble:

> As I urged you when I went into Macedonia, stay there in Ephesus so that you may command certain people not to teach false doctrines any longer or to devote themselves to myths and endless genealogies. Such things *promote controversial specu-*

> *lations* rather than advancing God's work—which is by faith. The goal of this command is love, which comes from a pure heart and a good conscience and a sincere faith. *Some have departed* from these and have turned to meaningless talk. *They want to be teachers of the law*, but they do not know what they are talking about or what they so confidently affirm.[9]

So, there seems to have been a problem in this specific church in Ephesus with a woman (or group of women) who were attempting to exert authority over others. This is what Paul is trying to help Timothy respond to. New Testament scholar Craig S. Keener helps shed some light on the situation:

> It is probably no coincidence that the one passage in the Bible prohibiting women teaching Scripture appears in the one set of letters where we explicitly know that false teachers were targeting and working through women. Paul's letters to Timothy in Ephesus provide a glimpse of the situation: false teachers (1 Tim. 1:6, 7, 19, 20; 6:3–5; 2 Tim. 2:17) were misleading the women (2 Tim. 3:6, 7). These women were probably (and especially) some widows who owned houses the false teachers could use for their meetings. Women were the most susceptible to false teaching only because they had been granted the least education. This behavior was bound to bring reproach on the church from a hostile society that was already convinced Christians subverted the traditional roles of women and slaves. So Paul provided a short-range solution: "Do not teach" (under the present circumstances); and a long-range solution: "Let them learn" (1 Tim. 2:11).[10]

Furthermore, please remember this: there is another category of person that Paul did not allow to teach as a way of exerting authority over a man—*men!* In other words, *no one* is allowed to exercise authority over anyone in the body of Christ. Why? Because Jesus commanded his disciples on two different occasions that they should never "lord it over one another" because "the greatest among you shall be your servant."[11]

There are numerous other problems related to our attempts to read this text without first understanding the cultural and religious environment of the city of Ephesus—which was the nexus of Artemis worship where the great temple to Artemis stood. This is also a huge issue in the book of Acts[12] when Paul is attacked by Artemis worshippers who, for over three hours, chant "Great is Artemis of the Ephesians!" in protest of his ministry.

Once you understand the complexities of Artemis worship, you will understand why the author says in 1 Timothy that "women will be saved in child-bearing." This is a direct reference to the reasons why women worshipped Artemis in the hopes that they and their child would not die during childbirth.

As for the passage in 1 Corinthians 14:34–35 where Paul seems to say:

> *Women should remain silent in the churches.* They are not allowed to speak, but must be in submission, *as the law says.* If they want to inquire about something, they should ask their own husbands at home; *for it is disgraceful for a woman to speak in the church.* (emphasis ours)

We must first recognize that Paul, as a Pharisee of Pharisees, would have known that the Law never commands "women should remain silent in the churches." But rather, that the Talmud does—in fact, the Talmud almost says verbatim, "it is a disgrace for a woman to speak" and that "a woman's voice is filthy nakedness."

Second, it must be noted that 1 Corinthians is a response to a letter written by the church in Corinth, which itself is a response to an initial letter sent by Paul that we no longer possess. And so, much of what is written in 1 Corinthians is Paul quoting things back to the church that they have said—perhaps even sarcastically—where he answers questions and responds to issues that they themselves have raised in their previous communications. Remember all that prosopopoeia stuff from Romans 1–4 and 9–11? Of course, you do! Well, the same thing is going on in 1 Corinthians.

Paul's response to their false teaching is this:

> *What?!* Did the word of God originate with you? Or are you the only people it has reached? *If anyone thinks they are a prophet or otherwise gifted by the Spirit, let them acknowledge that what I am writing to you is the Lord's command.* But if anyone ignores this, they will themselves be ignored. *Therefore, my brothers and sisters, be eager to prophesy, and do not forbid speaking in tongues.*[13]

A major issue with this passage arises from the fact that most modern English translations leave out the exclamation "What?!" which forces readers to believe that Paul himself forbids women to speak. This could not be further from the truth, as Paul does not agree with this statement, reminding the Corinthians to "acknowledge what I am writing to you is the Lord's command [not the Law]" and that they should *all,* women included, "be eager to prophesy and not forbid speaking in tongues"—something Paul had already affirmed earlier in this very same letter.

Remember, Paul's main goal throughout his writings is to warn against those who create divisions in the church, and that within the body of Christ, there are no dividing lines like "male and female."[14] This is a direct effect of the gospel, says the apostle. And so, unless Paul is openly violating his own gospel terms, something else is going on in 1 Corinthians, as we just demonstrated. In the very final paragraphs of Romans, then, Paul warns against those very same divisive people as follows:

> I urge you, brothers and sisters, to keep an eye on those who cause dissensions and offences, in opposition to the teaching that you have learned; avoid them. For such people do not serve our Lord Christ, but their own appetites, and by smooth talk and flattery they deceive the hearts of the simple-minded. For while your obedience is known to all, so that I rejoice over you, I want you to be wise in what is good, and guileless in what is evil. The God of peace will shortly crush [the Accuser] under your feet. The grace of our Lord Jesus Christ be with you (16:17–20).

Paul's emphasis here is again on watching out for "those who create division" with their "smooth talk and flattery"—i.e., the false teachers spreading a message of us vs. them, women vs. men, Jews vs. Gentiles, kosher vs. "unclean," gay vs. straight, slave vs. free, and so on. Like we just said, unless we believe Paul was among these—creating divisions between male apostles and female ones—then we must acknowledge that *something else* is going on when he writes what, on the surface at least, seems like a blatant disregard for the rules of his own game. In other words, if we are to take Paul seriously—an intellectual void of such blatant theological contradictions—then his rhetoric must also be acknowledged. Throughout this book, we hope we have made it clear what that "something" is—Paul quoting those he is in debate with over the nature of the gospel, often for the sole purpose of refuting their foolishness a few verses later. But to the wise, he offers this final doxology:

Now to God who is able to strengthen you according to my gospel and the proclamation of Jesus Christ, according to the revelation of the mystery that was kept secret for long ages but is now disclosed and through the prophetic writings is made known to all the Gentiles, according to the command of the eternal God, to bring about the obedience of faith—to the only wise God, through Jesus Christ, to whom be the glory forever! Amen (16:25–27).

EPILOGUE

Unveiling the Apocalypse of God

We began this book by admitting to some of the apostle Paul's complexities and problematic tendencies—the acknowledgment that he is difficult to comprehend, oftentimes bristly and sarcastic, and perhaps even arrogant and rude. As we close, we hope we have done our job in presenting another side to the New Testament's most prolific writer, not for the goal of whitewashing history, but of revealing it.

Because that is what apocalypse means—a revealing or unveiling. For Paul, the greatest apocalypse in the history of the world happened when God through Christ broke into time and space to unveil the truly good news, that though *all* stood guilty before a just God, *all* would be reconciled and redeemed, for true justice is in fact mercy. This is what the mind of the False Teacher cannot comprehend, and it is what so many Christians today fail to grasp.

For many, justice *is* wrath. Justice *is* retribution. The entire Protestant model of Justification rests upon this "fact"—that sinners must recognize their sinfulness in front of a retributive God of wrath and cry out for a savior. There is no other way to put it accept to say that this is the gospel of the False Teacher, which Paul says is no gospel at all.[1] A God of wrath and retribution is just like all the gods throughout history—hardly "set apart" or holy[2]—which makes him no God at all.

"God is love," says 1 John 4:8, which means that God's justice is loving. Even God's wrath—if we can call it that at all—is loving. To separate such qualities within God's self is to create a two-faced God. Given that the Romans already had a god of two faces—Janus, the god of duality—there seems little need for a Jewish or Christian God with such a similar nature.

But alas! Here we are, with a Christianity that, by and large, still uses Paul's epistle to the Romans to argue for such a deity. Which, given our exploration for how to properly read the letter, is quite the irony indeed! Donning the robes of the False Teacher, they eagerly and aggressively wield Romans 1:18–32 as a sledgehammer to condemn the LGBTQ+, stopping short of the inward finger pointing at their own hearts in Romans 2:1. With the gun-barrels of their gospel of wrath aimed at everyone else, they fail to realize that such a posture ensures their own violent destruction as they "store up wrath for themselves [...] for [falling short] of the glory of God" (2:1–5; 3: 23).

For those who refuse to take such an un-Christlike position, however, yet still struggle with this letter—and with Paul more generally—we hope this book has been a gateway into a whole new way to read the apostle. Not one removed from history, but one specifically informed by it.

We know that Paul's gospel was in danger of being written out of Christianity from its earliest days. Peter, James, and the Jerusalem church insisted that to be a Christian convert from outside Judaism, Gentiles had to take on Jewish markers and live by certain rites. Keeping the Sabbath and a kosher table were two of these, as was male circumcision. Not that this is the most pressing point to make about the issue, but could you imagine being an adult man undergoing a first-century circumcision? More to Paul's point on the matter, could you imagine forcing others to undergo such a traumatic procedure while violating the rules of your own religion behind closed doors? Or, as the apostle so bluntly puts it, "If you, though a Jew, live like a Gentile and not like a Jew, how can you compel the Gentiles to live like Jews?"[3]

Again, though, it seems too much of the Christian church is stuck in the ways of the False Teacher, so may this book be an excoriating rebuke of them, just as the letter to the Romans was 2,000 years prior. Because if we do not have a gospel that is for everyone—regardless of race, religion, socioeconomic status, gender, or sexual identity—then we do not have a gospel at all. The gospel of the false teachers came to Galatia dead on arrival. Years later, it came to Rome in the same way. And though it won over many with its fear-laden message and branding, it won over no one for Christ. As all high-control religious doctrines and dogmas do, it only brought the curse of death.

The antidote to such a curse is the gospel of Christ. It is a gospel stripped of all laws other than the law of love. It is a gospel for everyone. Full stop. It is a gospel that is truly "good news" because it puts Christ's compassion and mercy front and center, and relies solely on *his* solid faith. It is in such a faith that we trust, because when we do, we open endless possibilities of living, moving, and being in the world. When we trust in *this* gospel—the pure, unadulterated, and unsullied gospel—we move from crucifixion to resurrection. Christ has died and has been raised—so, too, have we been buried and brought to life by the God whose mercy endures forever and extends to all (11:32). "O the depth of the riches and wisdom and knowledge of God! How unsearchable are his judgments and how inscrutable his ways!" cries Paul. "For who has known the mind of the Lord?" indeed! No one could have imagined a God of such eternal mercy nor a hound of heaven so driven by his love for all that he will in fact rescue everyone from this cycle of sin and death. "For from him and through him and to him are all things," writes the apostle, and "to him be the glory forever."

Amen.

APPENDIX A

Romans 1:1–4:3 in Dialogue Form

Paul's Greeting

1 [1] Paul, a servant of Jesus Christ, called to be an apostle, set apart for the gospel of God, [2] which he promised beforehand through his prophets in the holy scriptures, [3] the gospel concerning his Son, who was descended from David according to the flesh [4] and was declared to be Son of God with power according to the spirit of holiness by resurrection from the dead, Jesus Christ our Lord, [5] through whom we have received grace and apostleship to bring about the obedience of faith among all the Gentiles for the sake of his name, [6] including yourselves who are called to belong to Jesus Christ, [7] To all God's beloved in Rome, who are called to be saints: Grace to you and peace from God our Father and the Lord Jesus Christ. [8] First, I thank my God through Jesus Christ for all of you, because your faith is proclaimed throughout the world. [9] For God, whom I serve with my spirit by announcing the gospel of his Son, is my witness that without ceasing I remember you always in my prayers, [10] asking that by God's will I may somehow at last succeed in coming to you. [11] For I am longing to see you so that I may share with you some spiritual gift to strengthen you— [12] or rather so that we may be mutually encouraged by each other's faith, both yours and mine. [13] I want you to know, brothers and sisters, that I have often intended to come to you (but thus far have been prevented), in order that I may reap some harvest among you as I have among the rest of the Gentiles.

Paul's Introduction of Theme

14 I am a debtor both to Greeks and to barbarians, both to the wise and to the foolish 15 —hence my eagerness to proclaim the gospel to you also who are in Rome. 16 For I am not ashamed of the gospel; it is the power of God for salvation to everyone who has faith, to the Jew first and also to the Greek. 17 The deliverance of God is revealed through the gospel by means of faithfulness for faithfulness; as it is written, "The Righteous One, by means of faithfulness, will live."

The Opposing Teacher's Introduction of Theme

18 "For the wrath of God is revealed from heaven against all ungodliness and wickedness of those who by their wickedness suppress the truth. 19 For what can be known about God is plain to them, because God has shown it to them. 20 Ever since the creation of the world his eternal power and divine nature, invisible though they are, have been understood and seen through the things he has made. So they are without excuse; 21 for though they knew God, they did not honor him as God or give thanks to him, but they became futile in their thinking, and their senseless minds were darkened. 22 Claiming to be wise, they became fools; 23 and they exchanged the glory of the immortal God for images resembling a mortal human being or birds or four-footed animals or reptiles. 24 Therefore God gave them up in the lusts of their hearts to impurity, to the degrading of their bodies among themselves, 25because they exchanged the truth about God for a lie and worshiped and served the creature rather than the Creator, who is blessed forever! Amen. 26 For this reason God gave them up to degrading passions. Their women exchanged natural intercourse for unnatural, 27 and in the same way also the men, giving up natural intercourse with women, were consumed with passion for one another. Men committed shameless acts with men and received in their own persons the due penalty for their error. 28 And since they did not see fit to

acknowledge God, God gave them up to a debased mind and to things that should not be done. [29] They were filled with every kind of wickedness, evil, covetousness, malice.

Full of envy, murder, strife, deceit, craftiness, they are gossips, [30] slanderers, God-haters, insolent, haughty, boastful, inventors of evil, rebellious toward parents, [31] foolish, faithless, heartless, ruthless. [32] They know God's decree, that those who practice such things deserve to die—yet they not only do them but even applaud others who practice them."

Paul's First Rebuttal: The Teacher's 'Wrath of God' Seen Instead as the Human Wrath of Judging

2 [1] Therefore you have no excuse, Every Person, when you judge others; for in passing judgment on another you condemn yourself, because you, the judge, are doing the very same things. [2] You say, 'we know that God's judgment on those who do such things is in accordance with truth.' [3] How do you think about it when you judge those who do such things and yet do them yourself: that you will escape the judgment of God? [4] Or do you disregard the riches of God's kindness and forbearance and patience—unaware that God's kindness is meant to lead you to repentance? [5] So by your hard and impenitent heart you are storing up wrath for yourself on the day of wrath, when God's righteous judgment will be revealed.

The Opposing Teacher's Restatement of the Standard View of God's Judgment

[6] ...Who will repay according to each one's deeds: [7] to those who by patiently doing good seek for glory and honor and immortality, he will give eternal life; [8] while for those who are self-seeking and who obey not the truth but wickedness, there will be wrath and fury. [9] There will be anguish and distress

for everyone who does evil, the Jew first and also the Greek, [10]but glory and honor and peace for everyone who does good, the Jew first and also the Greek. [11] For God does not respect mere appearance. [12] All who have sinned lawlessly will also perish lawlessly, and all who have sinned under the law will be judged by the law. [13] For it is not the hearers of the law who will be righteous in God's sight, but the doers of the law who will be justified.

Paul's Next Rebuttal: Gentiles Who Live by the Law Vs. Jews Who Do Not

[14] But when Gentiles, who do not possess the law, do instinctively what the law requires, these, though not having the law, are a law to themselves; [15] they show that what the law requires is written on their hearts, to which their own conscience also bears witness; and their conflicting thoughts will accuse or perhaps excuse them [16] on the day when God will judge the secret thoughts of all, according to *my* gospel, *through Jesus Christ.* [17] But if you call yourself a Jew and rely on the law and boast of your relation to God [18] and know his will and determine what is best because you are instructed in the law, [19] and if you are sure that you are a guide to the blind, a light to those who are in darkness, [20] a corrector of the foolish, a teacher of children, having in the law the embodiment of knowledge and truth,[21] you, then, that teach others, will you not teach yourself? While you preach against stealing, do you steal? [22] You that forbid adultery, do you commit adultery? You that abhor idols, do you rob temples? [23] You that boast in the law, do you dishonor God by breaking the law? [24] For, as it is written, "The name of God is blasphemed among the Gentiles because of you." [25] Circumcision indeed is of value if you obey the law; but if you break the law, your circumcision has become uncircumcision. [26] So, if those who are uncircumcised keep the requirements of the law, will not their uncircumcision be regarded as circumcision? [27] Then those who are physically uncircumcised but keep the law will condemn you that have the written code and circumcision but break the law. [28] For a person is not a Jew who is one outwardly, nor is true circumcision something

external and physical. [29] Rather, a person is a Jew who is one inwardly, and real circumcision is a matter of the heart—it is spiritual and not literal. Such a person receives praise not from others but from God.

First Dialogue of Paul and the Teacher—Paul as Questioner

3 *Paul*: [1] Then what advantage has the Jew? Or what is the value of circumcision?

Teacher: [2] Much, in every way. For in the first place the Jews were entrusted with the oracles of God.

Paul: [3] What if some were unfaithful? Will their faithlessness nullify the faithfulness of God?

Teacher: [4] By no means! Although everyone is a liar, let God be proved true, as it is written, "So that you may be justified in your words, and prevail in your judging."

Paul: [5] But if our injustice serves to confirm the justice of God, what should we say? That God is unjust to inflict wrath on us? (I speak in a human way.)

Teacher: [6] By no means! For then how could God judge the world?

Paul: [7] But if through my falsehood God's truthfulness abounds to his glory, why am I still being condemned as a sinner? [8]And why not say (as some people slander us by saying that we say), "Let us do evil so that good may come"?

Teacher: Their condemnation is deserved!

Paul Marshals Scripture Citations Before Climaxing His Argument

Paul: 9 What then? Are we any better off? No, not at all; for we have already charged that all, both Jews and Greeks, are under the power of sin, 10 as it is written: "There is no one who is righteous, not even one; 11 there is no one who has understanding, there is no one who seeks God. 12 All have turned aside, together they have become worthless; there is no one who shows kindness, there is not even one." 13 "Their throats are opened graves; they use their tongues to deceive." "The venom of vipers is under their lips." 14 "Their mouths are full of cursing and bitterness." 15 "Their feet are swift to shed blood; 16 ruin and misery are in their paths, 17 and the way of peace they have not known." 18 "There is no fear of God before their eyes."

The Core of Paul's Argument Against the Teacher: Universal Sinfulness Prompted Not Wrathful Judgment Under the Law but God's Unilaterally Saving Act in Jesus Christ

19 Now we know that whatever the law says, it speaks to those who are under the law, so that every mouth may be silenced, and the whole world may be held accountable to God. 20 For "no human being will be justified in his sight" by deeds prescribed by the law, for through the law comes the knowledge of sin. 21 But now, apart from law, the saving act of God has been disclosed, and is attested by the law and the prophets, 22 the saving act of God through the faithfulness of Jesus Christ for all who trust. For there is no distinction, 23 since all have sinned and fall short of the glory of God; 24 they are now justified by his grace as a gift, through the redemption that is in Christ Jesus, 25 whom God intended to be a singular act of atonement effective through that faithfulness in his blood. He did this to show his justice, because in his divine forbearance he granted amnesty for sins previously

committed; 26 it was to prove at the present time that God's justice is itself just in the very act of declaring everyone just from the faithfulness of Jesus.

Second Dialogue of Paul and Teacher—Teacher as Questioner

Teacher: 27 Then what becomes of boasting?

Paul: It is excluded.

Teacher: By what teaching? By that of works?

Paul: No, but by the teaching of faith. 28 For we hold that a person is delivered by faithfulness apart from works of law.

Teacher: 29 Or is God the God of Jews only?

Paul: Is he not the God of Gentiles also?

Teacher: Yes, of Gentiles also.

Paul: 30 If God is one—the God who will deliver the circumcised through fidelity—then he will deliver the uncircumcised through that same fidelity.

Teacher: 31 Do we then overthrow the law by this faith?

Paul: By no means! On the contrary, we uphold the law.

4 *Teacher*: 1 What then are we to say was found out in relation to Abraham, our ancestor according to the flesh? 2 For if Abraham was justified by works, he has something to boast about.

Paul: But not before God. [3] For what does the scripture say? "Abraham trusted in God, and it was reckoned to him as righteousness."

APPENDIX B

Romans 9:27–11:1 in Dialogue Form

9 *Paul:* [27] And Isaiah cries out concerning Israel, "Though the number of the children of Israel were like the sand of the sea, only a remnant of them will be saved; [28] for the Lord will execute his sentence on the earth quickly and decisively." And as Isaiah predicted, "If the Lord of hosts had not left survivors to us, we would have fared like Sodom and have been made like Gomorrah."

Teacher: [30] What then are we to say? Gentiles, who did not strive for righteousness, have attained it?

Paul: That is, righteousness through faith.

Teacher: [31] But Israel, who did strive for the law of righteousness, did not attain that law. [32] Why not?

Paul: Because they did not strive for it on the basis of faith but as if it were based on works. They have stumbled over the stumbling stone, [33] as it is written, "See, I am laying in Zion a stone that will make people stumble, a rock that will make them fall, and whoever trusts in him will not be put to shame."

10 [1] Brothers and sisters, my heart's desire and prayer to God for them is that they may be saved. [2] For I can testify that they have a zeal for God, but it is not

based on knowledge. 3 Not knowing the righteousness of God and seeking
to establish their own, they have not submitted to God's righteousness. 4
For Christ is the culmination of the law so that there may be righteousness
for everyone who believes. 5 Moses writes concerning the righteousness that
comes from the law, that "the person who does these things will live by them."
6 But the righteousness that comes from faith says, "Do not say in your heart,
'Who will ascend into heaven?'" (that is, to bring Christ down) 7 "or 'Who
will descend into the abyss?'" (that is, to bring Christ up from the dead). 8 But
what does it say? "The word is near you, in your mouth and in your heart"
(that is, the word of faith that we proclaim), 9 because if you confess with
your mouth that Jesus is Lord and believe in your heart that God raised him
from the dead, you will be saved. 10 For one believes with the heart, leading
to righteousness, and one confesses with the mouth, leading to salvation. 11
The scripture says, "No one who believes in him will be put to shame." 12
For there is no distinction between Jew and Greek; the same Lord is Lord of
all and is generous to all who call on him. 13 For "everyone who calls on the
name of the Lord shall be saved."

Teacher: 14 But how are they to call on one in whom they have not believed?
And how are they to believe in one of whom they have never heard? And how
are they to hear without someone to proclaim him? 15 And how are they to
proclaim him unless they are sent?

Paul: As it is written, "How beautiful are the feet of those who bring good news!"

Teacher: 16 But not all have obeyed the good news...

Paul: [For this reason] Isaiah says, "Lord, who has believed our message?" 17
So faith comes from what is heard, and what is heard comes through the word
of Christ.

Teacher: [18] But I ask, have they not heard?

Paul: Indeed they have: "Their voice has gone out to all the earth and their words to the ends of the world."

Teacher: [19] Again I ask, did Israel not understand?

Paul: First Moses says, "I will use those who are not a nation to make you jealous; with a foolish nation I will provoke you." [20] Then Isaiah is so bold as to say, "I have been found by those who did not seek me; I have shown myself to those who did not ask for me." [21] But of Israel he says, "All day long I have held out my hands to a disobedient and contrary people."

11 *Teacher:* [1] I ask, then, has God rejected his people?

Paul: By no means! I myself am an Israelite...

ABOUT THE AUTHORS

Keith Giles is a former pastor who left the pulpit over a decade ago to follow Jesus. He's been interviewed on CNN with Anderson Cooper, USA Today, Fox News, BuzzFeed and hundreds of other podcasts and radio programs. He has been a regular contributor to John Fugelsang's Sirius XM Radio show, "Tell Me Everything," as part of the weekly "God Squad" segment, and he is the founder and co-host of *Heretic Happy Hour*, and his solo podcast, *Second Cup with Keith*.

Keith is also the best-selling author of the 7-part "Jesus Un" book series focused on Deconstruction of the Christian faith, and the "Sola" book series focused on embracing the mystery of the divine. His latest book, *The Quantum Sayings of Jesus: Decoding the Lost Gospel of Thomas* is available now on Amazon.

Keith currently lives in El Paso, TX with his wife Wendy.

Matthew J. Distefano is a writer, business owner, and a graduate of CSU, Chico, dedicated to exploring the intersections of faith, culture, and social justice. He is the author of *The Wisdom of Hobbits* and *Mimetic Theory & Middle-earth* the host of the *High Minds* Podcast, as well as co-host of the *Heretic Happy Hour* podcast. Matthew engages in open and thought-provoking conversations that challenge conventional beliefs and promote inclusivity. His work centers on dismantling harmful ideologies and advocating for LGBTQ+ rights, racial justice, and a more compassionate understanding of spirituality. As a farmer and owner of Happy Woods Farm, Matthew also embraces the joy of cultivating the land and nurturing a sustainable lifestyle. With a unique blend of humor and insight, he invites readers to question, reflect, and ultimately find freedom in their beliefs.

Matthew lives in Chico, CA with his wife and daughter.

BIBLIOGRAPHY

Aristides. *The Apology of Aristides: Texts and Studies 1.* Translated from the Syriac. https://www.tertullian.org/fathers/aristides_05_trans.htm.

Bachman, Theodore E., Luther, Martin. *Luther's Words, Volume 35: Word and Sacrament I.* Minneapolis: Fortress, 1960.

Barth, Karl. *The Epistle to the Romans.* Translated by Edwyn C. Hoskyns. Oxford: Oxford University Press, 1968.

Beck, Richard. "Notes on The Deliverance of God: Part 1, Justification Theory." Experimental Theology. (January 14, 2010) https://experimentaltheology.blogspot.com/2010/01/notes-on-deliverance-of-god-part-1.html.

———. *The Slavery of Death.* Eugene: Cascade, 2014.

Becker, Ernest. *The Denial of Death.* New York: Free Press Paperbacks, 1973.

Boyd, Gregory A. *The Myth of a Christian Nation: How the Quest for Political Power is Destroying the Church.* Grand Rapids: Zondervan, 2005.

Campbell, Douglas A. *The Deliverance of God: An Apocalyptic Rereading of Justification in Paul.* Grand Rapids: Eerdmans, 2012.

Distefano, Matthew J. *From the Blood of Abel: Humanity's Root Causes of Violence and the Bible's Theological-Anthropological Solution*. Orange: Quoir, 2016.

———. *Heretic! An LGBTQ-Affirming, Divine Violence-Denying, Christian Universalist's Responses to Some of Evangelical Christianity's Most Pressing Concerns*. Orange: Quoir, 2018.

Dunn, James D.G. *The Theology of Paul the Apostle*. Grand Rapids: Eerdmans, 1998.

Giles, Keith. *Jesus Unarmed: How the Prince of Peace Disarms Our Violence*. Orange: Quoir, 2021.

Haldane, Robert. *Commentary on Romans*. Grand Rapids: Kregel, 1988.

Hamerton-Kelly, Robert G. *Sacred Violence: Paul's Hermeneutic of the Cross*. Minneapolis: Fortress, 1991.

Hart, David Bentley. *That All Shall Be Saved: Heaven, Hell, and Universal Salvation*. New Haven: Yale University Press, 2019.

———. *The New Testament: A Translation*. Second Edition. New Haven: Yale University Press, 2023.

Henry, Matthew. *Matthew Henry's Commentary on the Whole Bible, 6 Volumes*. Peabody: Hendrickson, 2014.

Hodge, Charles. *A Commentary on Romans*. Carlisle: Banner of Truth, 1983.

Hornblower, Simon and Spawforth, Antony, eds. *The Oxford Classical Dictionary: The Ultimate Reference Work on the Classical World*. 3rd Edition. Oxford: Oxford University Press, 1999.

Jersak, Bradley. *A More Christlike God: A More Beautiful Gospel*. Pasadena: Plain Truth Ministries, 2015.

Justin Martyr. First Apology. https://www.newadvent.org/fathers/0126.htm.

Keck, Leander E. et. al., eds. *The New Interpreter's Bible: A Commentary in Twelve Volumes*. Nashville: Abingdon Press, 2002.

Keener, Craig S. *The IVP Bible Background Commentary: New Testament*. Westmont: InterVarsity Press, 1994.

———. "Was Paul For or Against Women in Ministry?" Enrichment Journal. http://enrichmentjournal.ag.org/200102/082_paul.cfm.

Martyn, J. Louis. *Galatians: A New Translation with Introduction and Commentary*. The Anchor Yale Bible. New Haven: Yale University Press, 1997.

Peppiatt, Lucy. *Women and Worship at Corinth: Paul's Rhetorical Arguments in 1 Corinthians*. Eugene: Cascade, 2014.

Oakes, Peter. *Philippians: From People to Letter*. Cambridge: Cambridge University Press, 2001.

Sampley, J. Paul (ed.). *Paul in the Greco-Roman World: A Handbook*. Harrisburg: Trinity Press International, 2003.

Schnelle, Udo. *Apostle Paul: His Life and Theology*. Translated by M. Eugene Boring. Grand Rapids: Baker Academic, 2003.

Solzhenitsyn, Aleksandr I. *The Gulag Archipelago: 1918–1956: An Experiment in Literary Investigation*. Translated by Thomas P. Whitney. New York: Harper Perennial, 2007.

Stendhal, Krister. *Paul Among Jews and Gentiles: And Other Essays*. Philadelphia: Fortress, 1976.

Stowers, Stanley K. *A Rereading of Romans: Justice, Jews, and Gentiles*. New Haven: Yale University Press, 1994.

Talbott, Thomas. *The Inescapable Love of God*. Second Edition. Eugene: Cascade, 2014.

Taylor, Gordon Rattray. *Sex in History*. New York: Vanguard, 1954.

Wright, N.T., Wall, Robert W., et. al. *The New Interpreter's Bible: Acts; Introduction to Epistolary Literature; Romans; 1 Corinthians: 10*. Nashville: Abingdon Press, 2002.

Wright, Verdell A. "Progressive Christians can embrace Paul too." In Religion News Service. (December 12, 2017). https://religionnews.com/2017/12/12/progressive-christians-can-embrace-paul-too/.

ENDNOTES

EPIGRAPH

1. Wright, "Progressive Christians," para. 2.

The Problem of the Apostle Paul

1. What scholars seem to agree on is that Paul's first letter to Corinth was lost, as was their response. Thus, what we now call 1 Corinthians is really the third letter in the chain of correspondences (Paul's second).

2. See 2 Corinthians 12. By the way: we are not suggesting this. It is meant to be a joke. Do not take theology so seriously!

3. If you have ever listened to the *Heretic Happy Hour* podcast, or the now retired *Apostates Anonymous* podcast, you know exactly what we mean by this.

4. See Galatians 5:12.

5. Beck, "Notes on *The Deliverance of God*: Part 1," para 9.

6. 2 Peter 3:16.

7. Sorry to break it to you, Calvinists.

8. Scholars tend to believe that 1 Thessalonians was written sometime between 49–50 CE, with Romans following it up to a decade later. The Corinthian correspondences fall somewhere between these two epistles, while scholars are split on where to place Galatians. Some believe it predates 1 Thessalonians, while Paul K. Jewett, J. Louis Martyn, and others, date Galatians after. For our purposes, the dates are not at all important, though their order can indeed make a difference in how we approach the author.

9. Philippians 3:5–6.

10. If Paul's conversion happens between 31 and 36 CE, and the epistle to the Galatians is then written in 48 CE, a minimum of twelve years passes between the "big event" and his first letter. Paul's final letters will not come until perhaps 62 CE, roughly thirty years post conversion.

11. See Peppiatt, *Women and Worship in Corinth*.

12. See Galatians 3:28.

13. See 1 Corinthians 15:22.

14. Of course, neither N.T. Wright or David Bentley Hart are "new school" *anything*. Wright is a devout Anglican while Hart is an Eastern Orthodox philosopher and theologian, a tradition that predates Protestantism by roughly 1,500 years and is as ancient as Christianity itself.

Traditional Justification Theory and Its Many Pitfalls

1. For those who do not know, Alisa Childers is a YouTuber who constantly bemoans anything that diverts from "historic Christianity." The problem is that she herself is a Protestant, which is a belief system that only dates back 500 years.

2. Beck, "Notes on The Deliverance of God: Part 2," 32.

3. Ibid., 34.

4. This is the Arminian view.

5. This is the Calvinist view.

6. Beck, "Notes on The Deliverance of God: Part 2," 30.

7. Ibid., 31.

8. Jews realize this through Torah obedience, while Gentiles gain such knowledge through "innate moral law" available to everyone. See Romans 2:12–16.

9. Beck, "Notes on The Deliverance of God: Part 2," 33.

10. Campbell explains the process as follows: "The first phase in JT depends on individuals' detection within the cosmos of a series of propositions; this then establishes the conditions for any further progress toward salvation. Individuals must first grasp certain truths about God and then attempt to act on them (cf. Rom. 1:18-23). Specifically, they must grasp the truth of *theism*, of *monotheism*, of *divine transcendence* (that is, that this single God cannot be imagined, and so should not be), and the truths of this God's *retributive justice*. They must then grasp the specific concerns of this strictly just God with respect to human *heterosexuality* and *monogamy*, as well as, beyond these, *a fuller ethical system* (no envy, murder, deceit, and so on; cf. Rom. 1:29-31)" (Campbell, *The Deliverance of God*, 39).

11. A favorite phrase among Calvinists is "filthy rags." See Isaiah 64:6.

12. Campbell, *The Deliverance of God*, 44.

13. Ibid., 45.

14. Not to mention, ontological separation from the God who monotheistic Christians say is the glue that holds the universe together is a metaphysical and logical absurdity.

15. Campbell, *The Deliverance of God*, 62.

16. 1 Corinthians 15:22.

17. Beck, "Notes on The Deliverance of God: Part 3," para. 9. See also 1 Corinthians 13:4–5.

18. For more on mimesis, mimetic theory, and the anthropology of René Girard, see Matthew's book, *From the Blood of Abel.*

19. Campbell, *The Deliverance of God*, 76.

20. 1 Corinthians 15:22.

21. 1 Corinthians 15:22; Romans 11:32.

22. We have personally witnessed this type of behavior from Protestants (typically Calvinists) who insist that this is the only way to know someone is saved—*did they cry out for a savior after being tormented by their recognition of their sin?*

The Traditional Reading of Romans 1–4

1. No matter your view of Romans, it cannot be denied that Paul indeed quotes his scriptures creatively and often out of their original context. As the now popular joke goes, "Paul would fail most seminary Hermeneutics 101 courses."

2. Campbell, *The Deliverance of God*, 347–50.

3. Ibid., 342.

4. Ibid., 347.

5. Ibid., 367.

6. Solzhenitsyn, *The Gulag Archipelago*, Vol. 2.

7. For our Protestant readers, this is a Jewish book that rails against "those sinful" Gentiles, but is not found in your bibles.

8. Beck, "Notes on The Deliverance of God: Part 7."

9. We understand that the term "homosexuality" is outdated and brings with it unneeded baggage, given it was first used as a psychological diagnosis beginning in 1952. However, because it is still used within Christian circles—typically by those who are *not* LGBTQ+ affirming—we will be using it from time to time.

10. Hornblower and Spawforth, *Oxford Classical Dictionary*, 720.

11. Galatians 3:28.

12. See Jersak, *A More Christlike God,* 183.

Backdrop to the Apocalyptic View

1. Weak (or moderate) intentionalism recognizes the importance of an author's intent, while allowing room for readers to derive their own meaning from a text.

2. Stowers, *A Rereading of Romans*, 1.

3. Acts 9:15.

4. Campbell, *The Deliverance of God*, 495.

5. Galatians 1:7.

6. Galatians 5:12.

7. Galatians 6:13.

8. Campbell, *The Deliverance of God*, 501. Incidentally, the very same type of messaging was commonplace in the earliest incarnation of the Church. According to Acts 15:1, for instance, "certain individuals" had come from Judea, teaching that salvation cannot come unless one is "circumcised according to the custom of Moses."

9. Galatians 1:7.

10. Acts 9:18.

11. Galatians 1:6.

12. Galatians 1:7.

13. Galatians 2:14.

14. Galatians 2:15–21.

15. Galatians 3:10.

16. Galatians 3:11.

17. Galatians 3:13.

18. Galatians 3:19–20.

19. Galatians 1:7.

20. Campbell, *The Deliverance of God*, 587.

21. For your reference, we have also included a script of Romans 1–4 and 9–11 in the Appendices.

EPIGRAPH

1. Campbell, *The Deliverance of God*, 760.

Romans 1:18–32

1. The Greek term ecclesia can have multiple meanings, including "church" or "assembly," but within Christian circles it can specifically mean "called out ones."

2. It is noteworthy that Paul likely wrote this epistle to the Roman church from *Corinth*, a city where prostitution, pagan idolatry, and sexual immorality were quite widespread. Incidentally, it can be argued that Rome was even worse in this regard. Hundreds of temples to a variety of pagan deities were scattered everywhere. Pagan sexual worship practices were commonplace. Rome was the capital city of idolatry and pagan fertility rites, which is what Paul kicks off his letter describing (in typical Judaizing terms). But why does he do that? This is the key question we should be asking ourselves.

3. Again, in all actuality, we should not be using the term "homosexuality" at all, as it is an outdated term that has historic ties to being used as a mental health diagnosis.

4. Aristides, *The Apology of Aristedes*, sec. 2–4.

5. Justin Martyr, *First Apology*, Ch. 27.

6. Henry, *Matthew Henry's Commentary on the Whole Bible*, Isaiah 57.

7. Haldane, *Commentary on Romans.*

8. Hodge, *Commentary on the Epistle to the Romans*, 41.

9. It should be noted that we do not know any person who is gay because of worshipping idols through sexual intercourse. Do you? Maybe these people exist—we doubt it—but we would also venture to say that most of the people who identify as LGBTQ+ today did not "end up that way" because they used to engage in pagan sexual practices in the temples of Zeus, Artemis, or Cybele. Again, we suppose it *is* possible ... but let us be real! Further, we do not even know any LGBTQ+ people who are attracted to people of the same sex *because* they deny that God exists. In fact, the reality is just the opposite; we know many people who identify as LGBTQ+ who profess faith in Christ and who even demonstrate the heart and character of Jesus. They do not engage in, "shameful desires of their hearts" any more than our straight Christian friends do.

10. As we noted earlier, of course Paul did not think in these terms, as such sociological categories did not exist in antiquity.

Romans 2

1. Luke 21:3–4.

2. Luke 20:46–47, emphasis ours.

3. See John 8:7–11.

4. See Matthew 7:1–5.

5. In a most ironic fashion, any Christian who quotes Romans 1:18–32 to condemn the LGBTQ+ community is falling into the same trap that Paul set 2,000 years ago.

6. See Galatians 2–6 for more on this dispute in the early church.

7. These included, but were not limited to, male circumcision, keeping a kosher table, and adhering to the Sabbath.

8. Campbell, *The Deliverance of God*, 542.

9. Galatians 3:7, 26, 29, DBH.

Romans 3–4

1. Campbell, *The Deliverance of God*, 576.

2. Hamerton-Kelly, *Sacred Violence,* 78–80.

Romans 5–8

1. Campbell, *The Deliverance of God*, 708.

2. Hart, *The New Testament*, 296–97, Note P.

3. Ibid.

4. Ibid.

5. Ibid.

6. We realize not everyone became infected during the COVID outbreak, but for this analogy, imagine they did.

7. See also Ephesians 2:6.

8. In Hebrews 8:13, for instance, we read: "By calling this covenant 'new,' he has made the first one obsolete; and what is obsolete and aging will soon disappear." This raises the question: how can the old covenant Law be obsolete if New Testament writers—and even Jesus himself—said he did not come to abolish it and that it would remain until heaven and earth pass away? That is a big question, one we will answer in the following section.

9. 2 Corinthians 3:7–11, parentheticals ours.

10. Galatians 4:24–26, 30–31.

11. See also Galatians 5:18.

12. Galatians 6:2.

13. Galatians 3:29.

14. Matthew 5:17–18.

15. John 19:30.

16. John 17:4.

17. Wright, N.T. "NT Wright: Coronavirus Part of End Times Prophecy? God's Grief & Shock." *100Huntley*. YouTube. https://www.youtube.com/watch?v=J384Gx9nbkw.

18. See also Matthew 6:10.

19. Hart, *The New Testament*, 303, Note Y.

20. See Luke 23:34.

21. See John 20:21.

Romans 9–11

1. See 1 John 4:8.

2. See Genesis 25–27.

3. Hart, *The New Testament*, 306, Note AD.

4. Ibid., 311, Note AJ.

EPIGRAPH

1. Barth, *The Epistle to the Romans*, 527.

Romans 12

1. *Metanoia* is the Greek word we translate to "repent," and means "a change of mind" or "a change of one's thinking."

2. *Koinonia* is a Greek term for "fellowship" or "communion."

3. Mark 10:42–45.

4. Luke 22:25–27.

Romans 13

1. "Of God" is not found in the original Greek text.

2. Remember, however, that there are various understandings of "wrath," and that throughout his letter to the Romans, Paul distances his theology from the wrath-imbued gospel of the False Teacher, opting instead for a version of wrath that more anthropological than theological. In other words, the wrath of God is closer to what our friend Bradley Jersak describes as tossing a hammer into the air and having it land on our own head (Jersak, *A More Christlike God*, 183).

3. For more on this radical shift away from the nonviolent teachings of Jesus to the corruptions introduced by Constantine, see Keith's book *Jesus Unarmed: How the Prince of Peace Disarms Our Violence.*

Romans 14

1. 1 Corinthians 8:4–9.

2. See, also, Philippians 2:10–11.

Romans 15

1. Philippians 2:1–8.

2. See Acts 23:6.

3. See Acts 2:44–45.

Romans 16

1. Hart, *The New Testament*, 317–18, Note AS.

2. Ibid.

3. Of course, we say this with the full recognition that the gospel itself would have never left the tomb of Jesus had it not been for women! So, there is *that*.

4. Acts 9:36.

5. Acts 18:2–26.

6. Acts 16:14–40.

7. Philippians 4:3.

8. 1 Timothy 2:12.

9. 1 Timothy 1:3–7, emphasis ours.

10. Keener, "Was Paul for or Against Women," sec. 6, para. 2.

11. See Matthew 20:26–28.

12. Specifically, Acts 19:28.

13. 1 Corinthians 14:36–39, our emphasis.

14. Galatians 3:28.

EPILOGUE

1. Galatians 1:7.

2. The Greek term *hágios* (ἅγιος) means "set apart," "sacred," or "holy."

3. Galatians 2:14.

To contact Matthew J. Distefano or Keith Giles
for speaking engagements, please visit quoir.com.

Many Voices. One Message.

quoir.com

Made in the USA
Coppell, TX
31 January 2026

70526783R00114